The 3 Reasons Why
Book of Money & Business

Inspire. Educate. Entertain.

By 3RW & Ryan Stabile

www.3reasonswhy.com

See more reasons for everything at:

www.3ReasonsWhy.com

The 3 Reasons Why Book of Money & Business

First Edition.

Dedication

For all of those who seek knowledge.

Table of Contents

Introduction

The human race and our insatiable pursuit of knowledge is a tale that begins at the dawn of time. For better or for worse, seeking knowledge is hardwired into the human brain.

In fact, our quest for knowledge has historically often gotten the human race into trouble from the very beginning. Whether it be partaking in the forbidden fruit or the inquisitive cavemen of the prehistoric period who had to *know* which dinosaurs were herbivores and which were carnivores through a fatal series of trial and errors, *knowing* and *not know* can sometimes mean the difference between life and death.

Yet, still, the human race persists in *knowing things.*

Once our ancestors had their food, shelter and basic survival necessities fulfilled, they had the luxury of kicking back to relax as they pondered the mysteries of the universe.

The human race's biggest nemesis on their quest for knowledge has always been that daunting three letter word: why?

Everywhere you look, there is a potential "why?". While it would be difficult to go through life and ponder "why?" at every turn, sometimes you need to just kick back, relax and ask yourself all of those little questions. Only by asking the questions will you find the reasons for "why?". Those reasons are the only way that the human race can grow, learn and evolve beyond a prehistoric caveman. Because the more you know, the more you grow.

At 3RW, we believe that there are no stupid questions, only superfluous answers. A thirst for knowledge should not be oversaturated, like the constant barrage of information on the internet, or teased with just a few droplets of wisdom that only serve to intensify your thirst. 3 reasons are all you need to answer any "why?" and *The 3 Reasons Why Book of Money & Business* is your secret weapon in the fight against "why?".

Find out more of the 3 reasons behind life's biggest and littlest mysteries at the world's largest source for knowledge, www.3ReasonsWhy.com.

MONEY

3 Reasons Why Warren Buffet is so rich

Warren Buffet, CEO and largest stakeholder in Berkshire Hathaway is a philanthropist and entrepreneur. In 2008 he had the honor of being cited as the world's richest person. That takes some doing! You would think that someone who had accrued so much wealth would lavish money upon themselves. However, that doesn't appear to be Warren Buffet's style. So, just how do you defy global financial crises?

Here are three reasons why Warren Buffet is so rich.

Reason 1: He is frugal

It is a widely accepted fact that money generates money, and that the people who have the biggest bank balances are notoriously careful and thrifty with their cash. They are shrewd. Whereas conversely with very little funds and zero assets often throw their money away on trivial items, Warren Buffet ensures that every cent works hard for him and is accounted for. He is living proof that you can do good deeds with your money, while still maintaining full fiscal discipline.

Reason 2: He made smart investments

It would seem that Buffet wasted no time after leaving school. He made some incredibly smart investments very early in his career, and by the age of twenty had saved almost ten thousand dollars. Given how that was in the 1950's, that was an incredibly large sum of money for the time and would equate to somewhere in the region of one-hundred thousand dollars in today's money. He then continued to make investment after investment. Seemingly having the golden touch.

Reason 3: He took lessons in public speaking

Buffet appears to have been miles ahead of the game in terms of recognizing the power of public speaking. Very few people would associate mastering this art with wealth creation. However, the confidence that he gained enabled him to successfully eliminate any barriers that he encountered.

There can be no doubt that Warren Buffet's life story is incredibly compelling. Anyone determined to accumulate stratospheric levels of wealth would be wise to study this master.

3 Reasons Why capitalism has proven to be the most successful economic system

There are many different kinds of economic systems used around the world today. One of them is capitalism, and it is by far considered the most successful economic system. Capitalism is an economic system being used by various countries across the globe. Adam Smith is the father of capitalism and was responsible for laying down the basic foundations of it in his book titled "The Wealth of Nations." Unlike other economic systems, businesses have the upper hand under capitalism.

Here are the reasons why capitalism has proven to be the most successful economic system.

Reason 1: Beneficial for economic growth

Countries need a progressive economy in order to develop and rise to the ranks of the rest of the world. Capitalism is considered very beneficial for economic growth. To start, firms in a capitalist economy will produce in-demand goods and the pressures will lead them to cut costs and at the same time avoid waste. This is highly efficient. Firms and individuals face incentives, which will motivate them to work harder and be more innovative. This results in higher real GDP and eventually provides better standards of living.

Reason 2: Decreased government interference

Capitalism is a successful economic system because the government can only interfere and regulate the businesses minimally. This way, capitalism is a major advantage to businesses because they're not held hostage by the rules of the government. However, there's monopoly power which means that businesses that privately own a capital will have monopoly of power over products. In such cases, firms can exploit their privilege and charge higher for their products or services.

Reason 3: Continual improvement

Capitalism puts businesses in high competition with one another, with the top dog making the most money. This model forces businesses to continually improve their products and services in order to obtain the most customers. May the best business win!

Capitalism has proven to be the most successful economic system. It is beneficial for economic growth, decreases government interference and forces businesses to continually improve their products and services in order to survive.

3 Reasons Why Flat taxes for all is not practically feasible

When people talk about flat taxes they refer to a kind of tax system where everybody pays uniform taxes regardless of their income level. This is contrary to the United States' present system which follows a progressive tax where people who earn higher income pay higher taxes and those who earn lower income have lower taxes as well. There are many pushing for a flat tax system in the U.S. but it continues to follow the progressive tax system.

Here are the reasons why flat taxes for all is not practically feasible.

Reason 1: Unfair to the poor

If people pay flat taxes, those who earn more and less will be paying the same taxes. For example, if you have low income and you buy the same item as the one who earns more, you'll be paying the same taxes but in the end you'll have less money while the one with the higher salary will still have enough. This could be very unfair to low-income families because they often struggle to make ends meet.

Reason 2: Exemption on unearned income

Many argue that the lower and middle classes will be burdened if a flat tax system will be implemented especially when deductions will be removed and the tax base is expanded. That's because unearned incomes like those in the form of interest or dividends will be exempted. Some believe that in this manner, the working class will be supporting those who are rich.

Reason 3: Widen wealth inequality

A flat tax system will not be practically feasible at all because it will only widen wealth inequality. It may simplify the tax code but it will be at the expense of those who earn less. Further, those who oppose the flat tax system point out that it may give wealthy individuals the chance to duck paying taxes on some of their income. Some proposals on flat tax include exemption on investment income and many see these as very favorable to the rich.

Flat taxes for all is not practically feasible because it will be unfair to the poor and favorable for the rich. It includes exemption on unearned income and this will result in a wider wealth inequality in society.

3 Reasons Why is American Express is one of the most expensive cards to use

American Express has long since been one of the leading and most expensive cards to use. Even with the emergence of many rivals in the industry, Amex remains at the top of its game. It never fails to offer the best deals on credit cards such as releasing its most elite card ever called the Centurion Card or The Black Card.

Here are the reasons why American Express is one of the most expensive cards to use.

Reason 1: Invite-only card

American Express isn't for everybody. That's because the company is very careful when it comes to selecting the right customers to offer their cards to. Take, for example, their most expensive card, the American Express Centurion Card. You can't just visit the company and ask for this card because it is only available per invite-only. This means that you can never have this card unless Amex itself sends you your exclusive invitation.

Reason 2: Very expensive fees

Although American Express never really revealed the full details as to how people get invited, some information can be found on their website. Some AMEX cards have an annual fee of up to $2,500. Some cards require a payment of up to $5,000 just to open an account, after being invited, of course. Every year, American Express sends invites to the filthy rich who are lucky enough to meet their criteria, especially those who can really afford to pay the said fees.

Reason 3: Exclusive perks

The most expensive card goes with the most exclusive perks. The American Express Centurion Card has a minimum annual spending of $250,000 and that's more than a lot for the average American. For the filthy rich, well that's more than enough for them to afford flight upgrades or booking a complimentary hotel room at a short notice. There's also a 24-hour concierge available and even a personal shopper in case you need one.

American Express offers some of the most expensive credit cards because their targeted toward the uber rich. It is available on an invite-only basis and comes with very expensive fees, however, it also offers exclusive perks no other company can.

3 Reasons Why your credit score is extremely important for your financial health

Many people live on credit, including students and a majority of professionals. A good credit score can be very beneficial, especially when you need to buy something you can't afford to pay for in cash. The credit score is the three-digit number that's calculated from your credit report. A good credit score is somewhere around 720 or higher. Anywhere below that means you're scoring poorly.

Here are the reasons why your credit score is extremely important for your financial health.

Reason 1: It will determine your creditworthiness

Your credit history, including your credit score, will determine your creditworthiness. This means that banks and even your future employees, especially if you intend to work for the government, will check whether or not you're worthy of receiving a loan or credit card. Creditworthiness is your key to a good financial life and will benefit you until you grow old.

Reason 2: A loan when you need it

Do you want a brand new car? Do you want to buy a house? Do you want to start a business? You can make all of these possibilities realities by having a good credit score. Banks or financing companies will loan you the amount you need without a second thought once they see your excellent credit score. This is one of the many reasons why people are very cautious not to taint their credit score. It's difficult to loan a huge amount of money if you don't have a clean record.

Reason 3: Higher credit card limit

A good credit score will impress lenders and prove to them that you deserve more benefits such as increasing your credit card limit. You can apply for this increase from creditors while some simply add the additional limit automatically as a reward for your excellent credit score. This is beneficial on your part because with the increase, you'll also earn additional points on your high credit score.

3 Reasons Why you should invest in stocks

If you're looking around for the best place to invest your money in order for it to mature, stocks are more often than naught your best bet. But don't go investing right away! Buying stocks takes quite a bit of research beforehand, but the gains are some of the best available on the market today.

Here are three reasons why you should invest in stocks.

Reason 1: A better place for money

With CD accounts and IRA's interest at an all-time low (1% or less), stocks provide a much better return on investor's money. The stock market can offer 50% or more growth of invested income depending on how much you invest and low long. The stock market is not nearly as unstable as people think, either. In fact, it's actually quite predictable. Do your homework and watch the stocks closely for up to a month before you decide to invest, and even then, buy a stock which is a safe-bet for your first investment.

Reason 2; The strategic gamble

While stocks provide investors with huge gains in some cases, they can also often lead to a negative return in the long run. This is why it's important when investing in stocks to carefully watch the stock market.

When saving for retirement, stocks are after a much better bet than any 401K. with the more money you invest and the longer you give your stocks time to grow, the bigger your returns will be when you eventually retire. It's best to pick your stocks wisely and then pick a certain date you plan on withdrawing your money from the stock market. Meanwhile, never take your eyes off of your stocks – if they begin to crash consistently, get your money back before it's too late!

Reason 3: Do your research!

Investing in a well-researched stock could provide big gains for individuals willing to take the risk. Careful investments will include sure-bet stock growths, such as Google and Facebook, but you may also want to look into cheaper stocks which have huge potential to grow, such as lesser known companies or those who have just entered the stock market in order to see some real, exponential growth.

In conclusion, the stock market may be the best place to invest your money, certainly a better option than a CD or IRA, but it is not without its risks. Whether you're saving for retirement or just want to make a little extra cash in the short term, the stock market will provide some of the best returns available today.

3 Reasons Why the Casino always wins in Gambling

We all dream of winning it big. For many Americans who travel to casino destinations every year with a handful of disposable income, such as Las Vegas, they have no doubt in their mind that they are going to lose. But the idea of getting something for nothing is a fantastic fantasy, however, that it keeps scores of middle-class running back to the casino time and time again. In this article we will prove why the only way to get rich is through good, old-fashioned hard work and why the casino (house) always wins in gambling.

Here are three reasons why the Casino Always wins in gambling.

Reason 1: The odds are stacked

Even in a game where you have a 50% chance of winning, the casino will still win over time due to the law of large numbers. Unfortunately, craps is the only such casino game with decent odds, and even that is, well, a craps-shoot. Most games in casinos, slot machines especially, have such a small percent in favor of the gambler that there is virtually no way you can win large amounts of money. Casinos know that. Gamblers, for the most part, know that as well.

Reason 2: The casino knows their games better than you

Casinos, in a sense, invented the games that they allow people to play inside their businesses – and make no mistake, they are businesses. Not the game themselves, but the casinos knows all of the odds of each table, how many decks of cards, when to sort the cards – they even program their own slot machines. In order to even have the slightest chance of winning at casino games, gamblers would have to know all of those same odds – and how to beat them.

Reason 3: Casinos don't have to pay

Here is a little known fun fact about casinos – they never have to pay you your winnings. Take the story about Phil Ivey, for example, who won 7.7 million pounds from Crockfords, a casino in England. The casino determined that Phil Ivey was cheating (he wasn't) and only payed him his original stake. Ivey sued Crockfords and lost.

When we willingly hand over our cash for chips – a non-currency with no value – we should never really be surprised when the casino should suddenly decide that they do not want to recognize the value of their own chips.

3 Reasons Why you should care about bitcoin

Even Al Gore has shown his adoration for the emerging new digital-only currency invented by economist Satashi Nakamoto in 2008 and implemented in January 2009. It is a peer-to-peer currency which you will never be able to touch with your hands, and it's on a path for world domination.

Here are three reasons why you should care about bitcoin.

Reason 1: Everyone is using it

For many people, their first run in with bitcoin is during the checkout at one of their favorite online stores. Even many retail stores now have an option where you can pay using bitcoin, and it won't be long before Amazon even adopts the peer-to-peer currency.

Yes, the logo may look like a power-up in a Nintendo game, but that doesn't devalue the currency one bit. While bitcoin has seen a steady rise in its value since being put into action in 2009, as predicted with any emerging, international currency, it has fluctuated rapidly. At the date this article was written, one bitcoin (BTC) is the equivalent of $300 US dollar.

Reason 2: It's secure

Bitcoin uses unique 64-character address IDs for every transaction. Bitcoin does not use traditional bank accounts. Instead, everyone who uses bitcoin shares the same bank account. Additionally, bitcoin users can only make, or receive transactions through one-time-use transaction IDs. Confused? Bitcoin is breaking the rules of basic economics. In order to start using bitcoin, you'll need to download the entire database bitcoin transactions, which is roughly 30 gigabits, although other options are currently being developed.

Reason 3: It's fair

If you're one of the millions of American's who were livid after the bank bailout a few years back, or if you've racked up more than your fair share of superfluous fees with your checking account, then you will enjoy bitcoin.

For these same reasons, it's predicted that the big bankers will do everything they can to obstruct the inevitable rise of bitcoin's popularity, although only time will tell.

The 3 Reasons Why Book of Money & Business

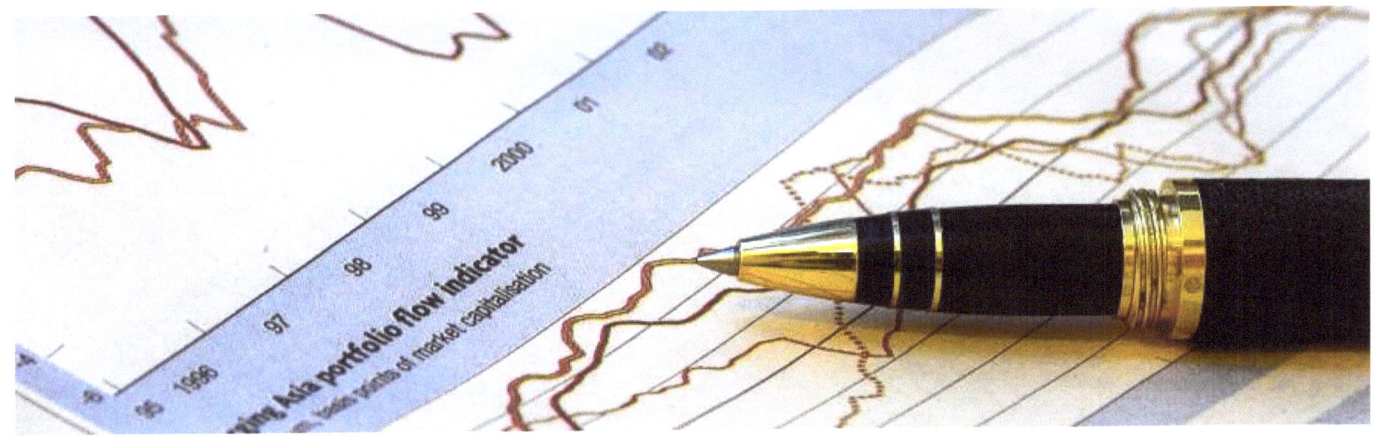

3 Reasons Why the stock Market exists

Why does the stock market exist? Have you ever stopped to ask yourself that question? You probably vaguely know that it has something to do with the economy, but that's often as far as some people's knowledge goes on the subject. Well, to help you understand, here are 3 simple reasons why the stock market exists:

Reason 1: To make money

The stock market provides a structure for regulated exchanges between investors to take place. Investors can buy and sell stock shares in public corporations where company owners can acquire equity investment. The stock market allows company operators to gain new cash from debt and make private or public investments.

Reason 2: Who it benefits

By making a company public, the company is able to get a huge infusion of equity cash. It also allows founders and existing shareholders to cash out their shares of stock. As well as being beneficial to investors and shareholders, the company itself benefits from the money it raises as a result of issuing public shares.

Reason 3: Creating the stock exchange

The United States stock market dates back to 1792 when the New York Stock Exchange acquired its first traded securities, and in 1817, the constitution of the New York Stock and Exchange Board was adopted; which paved the way for the modern day stock market. Without those first pioneers, the stock market would not exist!

Some people will argue that it's not necessary to have a stock market. The benefits of international trade and allowing the public to invest in shares seem like good ones, and many will say that the economy would crash overnight if you just took away the stock market. As with most things, there are two sides to every story, but those who argue against it believe that there is a better way of going about things. You'll probably need to research the stock market for yourself more before you can come to your own conclusions.

3 Reasons Why social security number was invented

It's something you probably take for granted: having a social security number. But have you ever stopped to wonder why it was invented in the first place?

Here are 3 reasons why social security was invented.

Reason 1: The reason for its inception

When the social security number (SSN) was first invented in 1936, it was simply created for one reason: to track earning histories of workers in the U.S in order to determine Social Security benefit entitlement, and to compute benefit levels.

Reason 2: The expansion of social security numbers

Since its inception, the use of social security numbers has expanded greatly. In the present day, SSN is one of the most commonly employed number systems in the U.S. Almost every citizen of the United States has a number, so in both government and private sectors, it has become the main way of identifying an individual and finding out related information about them.

Reason 3: Specific reasons for each group of numbers

The first three digits of any social security number are the numbers that identify where you live. The next two digits were created as a way of organizing Social Security Administration files into sub-groups, in order to make them easier to deal with. The last four numbers of your SSN are assigned consecutively to increase manageability of data. So the numbers themselves became longer over time as their functions increased.

Just think how much more difficult things would be to process if you didn't have a social security number! In this day and age of using numbers as means of identification for every business account and interaction going, it might be easy to overlook just how beneficial such systems are. Social security numbers greatly increase administration procedures and allow national security to be at its best. So, you are not just a number – of course – but being able to be identified as one has certainly helped the smooth running of the United States!

3 Reasons Why Social Security tax is collected

When you see that Social Security tax has been deducted from your wages, do you ever stop to wonder why it is collected? If you don't know, maybe you should find out- after all, it's coming out of your wage packet!

Here are 3 reasons why social security tax is collected.

Reason 1: For retirement

Simply put, Social Security tax is collected to fund the Social Security program. In part, this program pays for the retirement of millions of United States citizens. When you come to retire, you will certainly want to know that you are being looked after!

Reason 2: For disability benefits

The taxes are also used to pay for disability benefits which, again, millions of Americans will claim. If someone you know has a disability or you have one yourself, it will be easy to see why it's so important that the state helps.

Reason 3: For fairness!

In a democratic world of equality, such things as the decision to fund retirement and health problems are a no-brainer. Many countries don't have such systems, and unfortunately it's only too easy to see how everyday people suffer as a result. By paying your Social Security tax, you're simply caring for yourself and everyone else. If you unexpectedly had an accident which left you disabled, you would certainly want to know that you had some funds now that you were unable to work in your old capacity. Similarly, after decades of hard work, you would probably think it was only right that the state contributed to your welfare in your retirement years.

Social Security tax is usually paid through payroll tax or self-employment tax. So the next time you see the deduction from your wages, rather than moaning about paying too much in taxes, maybe you could be thankful that you're doing your bit and be happy to know that you will be looked after.

3 Reasons Why the US economy crashed in 2008

When the US economy crashed in 2008, it was after a time of turmoil around the world. Far from being the only major economy to flat line, to its credit it was also one of the fastest to recover. With so many people across the country experiencing extreme financial hardship, it is little wonder that so much vitriol and blame was apportioned to those whom people felt were the most to blame. So, let's unpick it.

Here are 3 reasons why the US economy crashed in 2008.

Reason 1: It was part of the global crash

America does not adopt isolationist policies. It is outward looking and generally very welcoming. However, one of the downsides to trading in a global marketplace is that you become vulnerable to the same risks as everyone else. So, as the contagion spreads, you too find that you have been exposed to it. There is little doubt that American companies contributed to the crash. However, it would be reckless to peg the full blame on them.

Reason 2: Lehman Brothers

The very mention of the words Lehman Brothers is enough to send shudders down spines across the country. For indeed it was their collapse that started a domino effect which would reverberate around the world. Banks, and large financial institutions which had been trusted and respected by millions suddenly found themselves lambasted as one by one their dodgy practices were exposed.

Reason 3: The Housing Crisis

The Housing Crisis or American Subprime crisis was another major trigger. In a nutshell, people had been allowed to borrow way more than they could ever hope to repay without due diligence being carried out. This led to foreclosure after foreclosure as the entire sector collapsed.

3 Reasons Why 401K was invented

For many Americans 401k is the difference between financial security in retirement and an old-age seeped in misery and worry. Unlike a lot of IRS rules and regulations, section 401k of the Internal Revenue Code is actually designed for the benefit of the individual rather than the US Treasury. (Although, the treasury does ultimately gain from the inevitable tax windfall) So, in case this is all still a little confusing for you here are 3 reasons why 401k was invented:

Reason 1: To offer security in retirement

With workers able to invest up to $18000 per annum tax free (until the pension is collected) 401K was primarily set up to offer security in retirement and ensure that people who had done the right thing and worked hard all of their lives had a decent quality of life and were secure in their retirement. No-one wants to work all that time and then wind up unable to afford some of life's little luxuries, do they?

Reason 2: To raise taxes for the treasury

Okay, so there is had to be an ulterior motive. Regardless of how it chooses to dress it up it is not within the nature of any government to give the people something totally altruistically without expecting something in return. Although, it doesn't collect until the policy holder retires, the government is assured of a continuous stream of revenue as people hit the retirement age on a daily basis.

Reason 3: To reduce welfare dependence

This last point goes hand in glove with the second point. By ensuring that more and more Americans take advantage of this scheme, and save frugally for their retirement, the government is also keeping welfare spending to the minimum. Just think of a hypothetical situation with an increasingly ageing population if people hadn't taken out their 401K?

So, while the average American does benefit from having the policy in place, as usual it is the government that is the ultimate winner.

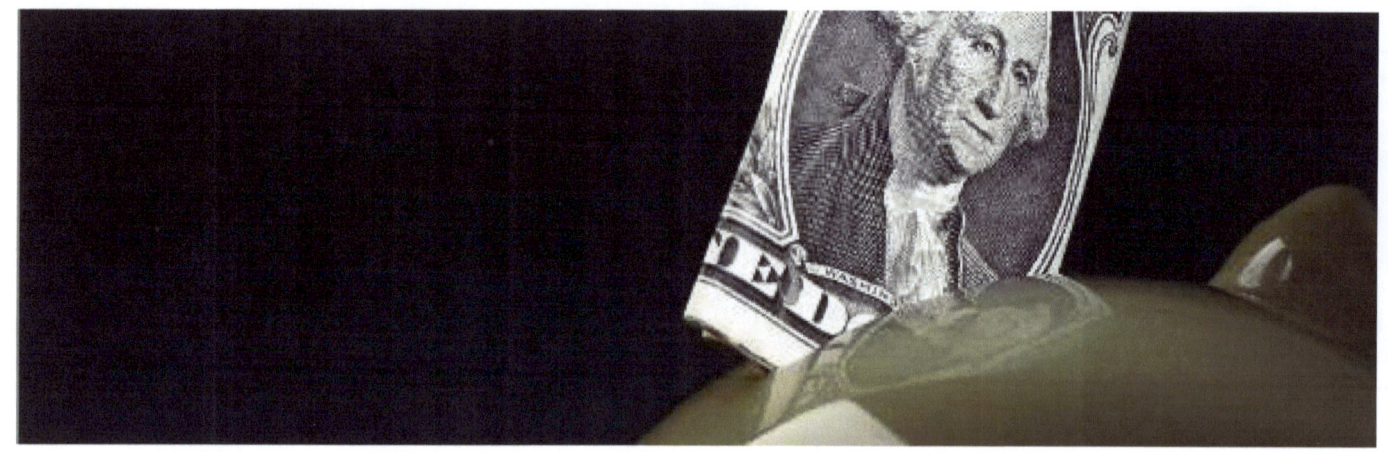

3 Reasons Why filing bankruptcy is not always a good idea

An unavoidable financial crisis can force any person or a company to file for bankruptcy. While some people file for bankruptcy simply for tax reasons, this is not always a good idea and will cause a financial rippling effects which will do more harm than good in the long run. Whatever your reasons are for filing bankruptcy, consider your options and think twice before filing for bankruptcy.

Here are the reasons why filing bankruptcy is not always a good idea.

Reason 1: Bad credit

Filing for bankruptcy may seem like the easiest way to get out of a financial crisis, but it will also result in bad credit. What will happen a year, five years or 10 years down the road? Will banks give you the loan you need to start a new business? Do you think that it will be easy to get investments in your next big venture? Filing for bankruptcy will leave you with bad credit that will discourage banks and investors from working with you and your money.

Reason 2: You lose your possessions

Once you file for bankruptcy, be ready to say goodbye to some of your most prized possessions. You'll lose and property which isn't exempt. However, exemptions may vary from one state to another. State laws govern a debtor's property in most states, and these laws protect only the fundamental possessions. The state wants you to pay back your debt in any way you can, why means you'll have to sell off most of your stuff.

Reason 3: You won't be free of debts

It's a common misconception that when you file for bankruptcy you'll be free from all debts. Although bankruptcy can remove many debts in the form of discharge, it has limits. For instance, discharge doesn't include debts that have to do with drunk driving, alimony, income taxes and divorce settlements among others. Remember that once a debtor is discharged, it will take another six years before he or she can obtain another discharge.

Filing bankruptcy is not always a good idea because you'll end up with bad credit, you'll lose your most prized possessions and still won't be free from all your debts.

BUSINESS

3 Reasons Why monopolies exist

When we talk about monopolies, we refer to a market structure wherein only a single seller is responsible for selling a particular unique item in the market – not the board game. In other words, it has no other competition being the sole seller. But why is it that there are countries that allow monopolies to occur?

Here are the reasons why monopolies exist.

Reason 1: It is advantageous to firms

Can you imagine starting a business wherein you have no competition? That's one of the benefits of monopolies. They will allow firms to grow and succeed. For instance, domestic monopolies can be dominant in their specific territories and, eventually, may penetrate the global market. This way, the country itself earns export revenues from the said firms. Further, the government can closely monitor businesses in monopolies and ensure they don't offer overpriced goods and services.

Reason 2: Research and development benefits

Many countries allow monopolies for research and development purposes. They study the growth of a particular firm and find out what contributes to its success or failure. The results of their research will serve as a guideline to improve products and at the same time lower the costs in the future. This is especially true with telecommunication and pharmaceutical companies.

Reason 3: Protects rights

Another reason is that monopolies exist is that they are an effective way to protect the rights of producers. As a sole firm running a particular business in a territory, you feel more secure. You have total control of the resources and are the only firm allowed to exploit them. Of course, there are restrictions, too, but once you're granted monopoly, it's understandable that you make use of such resources wisely.

Monopolies are still rampant in today's modern economy. That's because they are beneficial to a country's development. They are advantageous to firms, especially new or emerging ones. In addition, they can be used for research and development and in avoiding wasteful duplications.

3 Reasons Why 95% all of all new businesses fail

It's a dog eat dog world out there, and if you can't keep up with the competition, you'll be eaten alive. Most businesses come and go, however, why is it that some corporations set themselves up for success from the start and dominate the marketplace? Many new businesses simply cannot thrive in today's global market. As reported by CNBC, there are 400,000 new businesses opening every year but 470,000 are closing.

Here are the reasons why 25% of all new businesses fail.

Reason 1: Not enough market research

Regardless of if a new business fails because they lack the fund or if they cannot properly market their new products, the real culprit behind 95% of new businesses getting washed down the drain is because their founders simply did not do enough market research from that gates. Had a new business founder done their due diligence and properly researched everything about their industry before jumping right in, they would have realized that it requires a minimum of X amount of dollars in order to build a successful business in that industry.

Reason 2: Poor direction and understanding

Many new businesses fail because owners themselves don't have the full understanding of what they're getting themselves into. Instead of taking the time to study what business will best work with their target customers, many would jump into a venture simply because they believe it will bring in lots of money. This is a misconception and is oftentimes one of the reasons why many new businesses don't make it.

Reason 3: The wrong product or service at the wrong time

Sometimes when a new business fails, it is more due to the current state of the economy rather than the state of their products or services. This is still something that should be closely analyzed by entrepreneurs before starting a new business venture. Remember: research, test, succeed.

3 Reasons Why the Koch Family is among America's most successful in industry and business

The Koch family built one of America's largest business empires and today, they're considered one of the most successful families in the fields of industry and business. What makes them so popular, wealthy, and successful?

Here are three reasons why the Koch Family is among America's most successful families in the fields of industry and business.

Reason 1: They own Koch Industries Inc.

Companies owned by the Koch family manufacture a wide range of products supplied to numerous businesses throughout the United States. They have companies in over 60 countries with up to 100,000 employees, 60,000 of whom are in the U.S. Its companies include Flint Hills Resources, LLC; Georgia-Pacific, LLC; INVICTA; Molex Incorporated; Koch Pipeline Co., L.P. Koch Ag and Energy Solutions, LLC; and Koch Chemical Technology Group, LLC. Koch Industries also owns Koch Supply and Trading; Koch Minerals, LLC; and Matador Cattle Company.

Reason 2: Koch Family Foundations and Philanthropy

Having all that money makes the Koch family very active in the field of philanthropy. They founded the Koch Family Foundations and Philanthropy which supports many organizations and causes. They help foster entrepreneurship, provide scholarships, finance medical research, and support environmental projects. The family's foundations include the Fred and Mary Koch Foundation, Koch Cultural Trust, Charles Koch Foundation, Charles Koch Institute, and David H. Koch Charitable Foundation and Personal Philanthropy.

Reason 3: A very controversial family

Perhaps one of the reasons why the Koch family is successful is because they've overcome many controversies that haunt their family. Charles Koch father, Fred Koch, removed his eldest son from his will. Frederick was cut off because he stole traveler's checks as well as cash from their father. Also in 1998, the case of Koch vs. Koch Industries had their trial at the Topeka courtroom where Charles and David Koch prevailed over their brother Bill who referred to them as crooks. They ended their family feud in 2001.

The Koch Family is amongst America's most industrialists and businesspeople people because of their popularity and wealth. They're also known for their philanthropic works. Aside from these, the family is very controversial.

3 Reasons Why FeedForward is way better that Feedback

Businesses used to be fond of giving feedback to their employees. Nowadays, this is no longer the case. FeedForward is a new strategy which is being used by many companies to help their workers become more productive and active in the workplace. FeedForward refers to providing suggestions and tips to people that will help them improve their work in the future. It doesn't deal with what happened in the past by pointing out the mistakes of others. It's more about helping each other to be successful.

Here are the reasons why FeedForward is way better than feedback.

Reason 1: FeedForward is more effective

FeedForward is a far better and more effective technique when it comes to giving ideas. When you give feedback, you usually base it on what a person did or presented. You observe people's mistakes then give your reaction. Your suggestions afterward will be based on those mistakes. With FeedForward, you immediately provide the necessary suggestions to the person without going back to his or her mistakes. You no longer humiliate that person because of the mistakes he or she committed, but instead provide ways for improvement.

Reason 2: FeedForward focuses on the future

Feedback has a negative connotation to it. Many people don't like hearing feedback because they know they will be corrected for the wrongs they've done and sometimes even get embarrassed in front of others. It dwells more on the past than potential growth. FeedForward is more focused on the future. It is more motivating because you're working towards possible positive outcomes and not dwelling on what you weren't able to do before.

Reason 3: FeedForward focuses on goals

One of the perks of FeedForward is that it's more focused on goals instead of standards. A manager, for instance, identifies goals which best fit an employee's role. This way that employee will focus on what is expected of him or her. This will greatly motivate that person to work hard to achieve the goals laid out for him or her. Instead of simply providing corrections for the wrongs done, a manager will use FeedForward to ensure that employees are on the right track.

3 Reasons why your path to climbing the corporate Ladder might be different

We all start at the bottom when we break into a new career. Or do we? Is there some way to fast track the corporate ladder we all have to climb in order to make it to the top? Everyone's climb to corporate success is actually unique in its own way.

Here are three reasons why your path to climbing the corporate ladder might be different than others.

Reason 1: Different industries

Although most businesses in different industries follow the same corporate format, each path from the bottom to the top is unique according to each industry. Every company and industry has a layout that is unique to their market. Although this can sometimes be very subtle, climbing the corporate ladder in an agriculture business will be very different from that of a stock trading business.

Reason 2: Schmoozing

We all know how important networking is in every career. This is especially true when climbing the corporate ladder. It's not just important to get close to the people at the top, but it's even more important to win their affections and get on their good side. This way, you'll be the first person they think of the next time an opening for a promotion comes up. This is true in any industry and is the one thing that most jobs do actually have in common, regardless of what market you are in.

Reason 3: Your own path

You might choose to forget the whole corporate ladder altogether and follow your own path to success. if you ever should choose to diverge from the corporate ladder altogether by taking the knowledge and skills you possess and bridge out by starting your own enterprise, guess what? You start from the bottom of yet another corporate ladder in your new chosen industry. This is true of every new niche – as the newcomer, you must always start on the bottom, but that doesn't mean that you can use many of the same leads and networks you've developed over the course of your career. See? Networking helps, regardless.

As we can see from the three reasons above, climbing the corporate ladder to the top is never the same for any one individual. Rest assure that your path to the top will not be the same as the next persons.

3 Reasons Why self-publishing is changing the whole publishing industry

More and more are seeing authors self-publish their books. E-books are becoming more and more popular, but what does that mean for traditional publishing houses and how is self-publishing affecting the industry? Let's look at three reasons why self-publishing is changing the whole way the publishing industry works.

Reason 1: User friendly distributors

The advent of user friendly self-publishing distributors, such as Smashwords, Kindle Direct Publishing and Createspace, have put the power of publishing in the hands of the people. This is a modern marvel in the publishing industry, where previously authors could only get their work published by submitting treatments for their book to major publishing houses or winning over a literary agent.

Not unlike the shift in the music industry that happened over the last decade - where the popularity of music production software and in-home studios are now accessible to *every* musician on Earth – anyone can now become an author. Although that also means that, not unlike the music industry of today, the eBook market is now overflowing with plenty of *terrible* literature.

Reason 2: Vanity Publishing

Vanity publishing is where an author will pay a company, such as Author House or Xlibris, to publish their book and market their book. Although this is a terrific option for many who find it difficult to navigate the confusing sea of self-publishing distributors and their many different qualifications and requirements involved in publishing, vanity publishing houses often masquerade as authentic publishing houses – the only difference is that vanity publishers will charge for their services. This is not a bad thing, however, as vanity publishers also offer authors a wide range of distribution, their own ISBN, and some great marketing services, allowing authors to concentrate on the writing.

Reason 3: eBook accessibility

According to IBIS World Market Research, between 2009 and 2014, the Ebook industry has grown an average of 37% every year with a mean revenue of $4 Billion dollars. Let that soak in for a bit, because those are powerful numbers that will make even the most successful stock market gurus want to leave Wall Street and start writing Ebooks.

Where, previously, those who identified themselves as "readers" were forced to carry bulky, physical books with them, Ebooks have made reading accessible to virtually anyone. Anyone with a smartphone, tablet, or computer has access to billions of Ebooks and endless amounts of information.

Now that we can see how the advent of self-publishing has drastically changed the whole publishing industry, the only question is – can the stuffy old publishing houses of yesterday keep up, or will they go the way of the dinosaurs? Only time will tell, however, the fact that many already established publishing houses have already closed up shop is already a clue. If Random House and Penguin hope to keep up with the exponential growth of the publishing industry, they will have to continue to innovate in order to survive.

3 reasons why speed reading is an essential skill and how to increase your reading speed

If you aren't speed reading, you are cheating yourself out of your own time. This handy skill is especially important in college or any academic setting, but also an imperative skill for all facets of life.

Here are three reasons why speed reading is an essential skill and how you can increase your reading speed.

Reason 1: Quicker Comprehension

At its essence, speed reading is a method of learning information much quicker than traditional methods. Many speed readers claim to be able to take in over 1,000 words per minute, however, comprehension drops dramatically at that level. The key to speed reading is a balance between eye movement and reading comprehension. Experienced speed readers constantly adapt their reading speed to match the importance and difficulty of the content. Difficult content requires a slower reading speed, while simple content can be read much more quickly.

Reason 2: Only practice speed reading under the best conditions

In order to get the most out of your speed reading sessions, it's important to only read when you know you have enough mental energy to do so. Speed reading inherently requires you to be in a high-energy state. Therefore, like any intense activity, performance can be improved through a proper warm-up. It may sound silly, but try to get your heart rate up a bit by jobbing in place beforehand. When all else fails, there is always coffee or tea. Standing promotes blood flow, which increases alertness and energy levels. It also engages all your limbs, making it a more engaging activity. Of course, you don't have to always do this.

Reason 3: Different methods of speed reading

The pointer method is a great beginner technique to force your eyes to adapt to a faster reading speed. Grab a pen, chopstick or other thin stick-like object. Trace under the words and let the tip guide your eyes. The pen is just a guide; don't draw on the book. Trace at a pace that is 10 to 20% faster than your typical reading speed. Continually push yourself by speeding up once you've adapted. The pointer method has three distinct advantages, such as ensuring that you read at or near your current top speed. It also helps you maintain a consistent speed while reducing instances of you losing your place.

Once you reach a certain point in speed reading, you will naturally begin scanning the words both above and/or below the line you are reading. This will result in non-linear reading, or reading that doesn't follow the natural order of the words. It's basically an advanced form of block reading that extends vertically. At first, this will work as a form of previewing, rather than reading words, but with enough practice, you may develop the ability to read multiple lines simultaneously.

As with anything, practice makes perfect! You may be able to only read 400 words per minute at first, however, if you keep using these tools, you'll be able to read like an all-star in no time.

3 Reasons Why promotion and marketing are essential when self-publishing

Self-publish is one of the finer innovations of the 21st century, putting the power of information into the hands of the people for readers and writers alike. That doesn't mean that getting your book noticed will be easy.

Here are three reasons why promoting and marketing are essential when self-publishing

Reason 1: You won't be "discovered"

Why are large publishing houses so successful in selling their books? It's because of their massive marketing budgets. While self-publishing has allowed authors to reach many of the same distribution channels as the larger publishing houses, without a similarly lofty marketing budgets, self-publishing authors may find it difficult to sell their books.

For this same reason, publishing houses, as well as literary agents, very particular about who they sign.

Reason 2: You need a following

Have you ever bought a book – or seen a movie – just because you knew who had created it? The famous authors who have become household names have spent years, even decades, articulating their fanbase through constant quality releases. This level of loyal readers is almost always accumulated over a long period of time. You may be the next Hemmingway, but the chances of you being discovered and turning your first book into a "cult classic" are slim.

One of the most powerful tools self-publishing authors can have at their disposal is a dedicated website with an email list sign-up feature. While building this all-important email list, you are effectively building a following of loyal fans.

Reason 3: Don't be afraid to ask for help

It's almost impossible for new authors to accomplish all of the marketing for their book that traditional publishing do, especially most publishing houses have been doing this for decades.

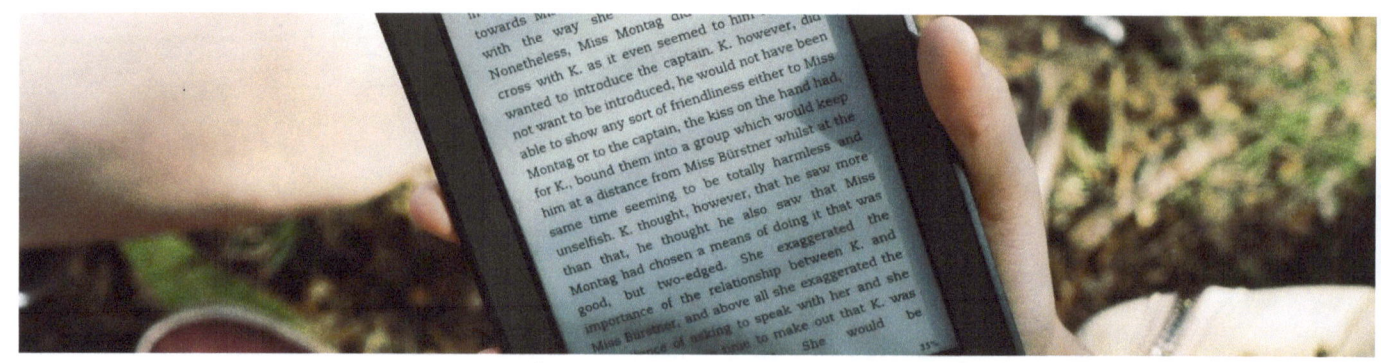

3 Reasons Why Q&A eBooks sell the best

Have you bought an eBook just to find an answer to a mundane question? Would you do so if I told you that an eBook on a subject which you were passionate about is priced at $0.99? These sort of eBooks, usually with an informative, "How to" title, are leading the way in bestselling eBooks right now.

Here are three reasons why Q&A eBooks sell the best.

Reason 1: Detailed answers to specific questions

eBooks provide an in-depth look at basic, yet often very specific questions. A lot of times these books contain some very unique research studies or information which is not available anywhere else. What you are essentially paying for is an expert opinion or instruction on how to do something very specific, usually written by an expert in that field. Think of it like investing in a mini-college course which you may study for at your leisure.

Reason 2: Fiction is a dime a dozen

There are literally millions of fantasy and romance eBooks available on the market for $0.99 (Romance is the second best-selling category of eBook). These obscure categories of fiction have a very generalized target audience, whereas Q&A eBooks have a very specific audience.

For example, "How to Make Money Writing Full-Time" has a clearly defined target audience and customer base. Here, we know that only aspiring writers will buy this book. The narrower the niche is, the easier it is to reach the audience of that niche.

Reason 3: The eBook market is exploding

Ten years ago, you would never have seen read these words: The eBook market is exploding right now. What we're seeing right now in the publishing industry is an explosion in the popularity of eBooks, and as a result, an increase in the quantity of self-published eBooks. IBIS World, who conducts market research on various industries, reports that the eBook industry averages $4 Billion annually and saw a growth rate of 37.4% from 2009 to 2014.

3 reasons why speed typing is an essential skill and how to type faster

Not unlike speed reading, speed typing is an invaluable tool in any professional writer's toolbox. This is especially true to those who churn a lot of content, because the faster you type, the more money you will make.

Here are three reasons why speed typing is an essential skill and tips on how you can quickly learn to type faster.

Reason 1: Your time is worth it!

Time is the one resource we have that is finite. If it takes you half an hour to send one email, then that is time that you'll never get back. For many occupations, the faster you type equivocates to the more money you'll make. Speed typing is a lifelong skill that will help in every facet of your life, regardless of what you do at your day job. Plus, speed typing is skill which you can continually improve upon your whole life. Do you need any more reasons to start speed typing?

Reason 2: Get cozy and go to work!

It should go without saying that you work better when you're more comfortable. The same goes for typing. Make sure you're sitting up straight, but allow your wrists to rest while your fingers are on the keyboard. Having them in the air inhibits your speed and is just plain uncomfortable.

Additionally, keep both feet on the floor and take breaks when needed. If your fingers or hands start to hurt, take a break! Straining yourself gets you nowhere, but pacing yourself will improve your strength. It takes time, but eventually you'll need to take fewer rest breaks.

Once you've gotten a decent feel for where the keys are laid out, eliminate the habit of looking down while you type. For one thing, it prevents you from visually editing your copy in real-time, meaning more mistakes and more time wasted editing in the end. You'll also learn the layout of the keys a lot faster since you are not taking any mental shortcuts.

Reason 3: Practice makes perfect!

The worst thing you can do is become complacent. Your typing skill can always get better as long as you're balancing how fast you type with how correctly you type. Test your speed routinely and set goals for the WPM you want to reach.

Once you've reached it, aim higher! Consider getting some coworkers or friends in on it and see who will reach the farthest. Whatever you decide to do, remember that typing is like any other skill out there: it requires practice, patience and time. Commit to improving it and you'll get fantastic results.

3 Reasons Why we get writer's block and how to beat it

We all have those moments where words just won't come easy. The muses are certainly a fickle bunch, however, the sooner you get to know what inspires and motivates you the better off you are in the long run. There are many ways in which you can find inspiration; most of them sound silly, but they work!

Here are three reasons why we get writer's block and how you can beat it.

Reason 1: You are uninspired or burnt out

If you're feeling a bit uninspired, try read inspiration quotes. Sooner or later you will find something that resonates with you. Pintrest is great for this, or just use Google images. Save the best ones in a folder on your computer and refer to them during any time you come down with a case of writer' block.

Word games like Boggle and Scrabble are also great for this and force your mind to think of letters and words in unconventional ways. If you need a quick little inspirational pick-me-up throughout the day, try relaxing with a cup of tea and a crossword puzzle. The results may surprise you.

Reason 2: Get back to the basics

In order to champion writer's block, you may want to get back to the basics. Listen to your favorite music from back when you were at the peak of your inspiration. Watch an old favorite movie of yours. Read your favorite parts from your favorite book. Get into a long conversation with someone you haven't talked to in a few years. But remember, it's important that you don't linger too long in a nostalgic state of mind, lest you begin to backtrack

Reason 3: Exercise and Meditation

If you're stuck on a one particular part of a writing endeavor, there are many things you can do to find your muse and jump start your brain. First, it is important to know your mind as well as your body. The best two weapons you can have in your fight against writer's block are exercise and mediation.

The great thing about exercise and meditation is that they provide prominent results in your body and mind instantly and you can continue to reap these benefits throughout the day. Unlike caffeine, the intense mental clarity provided by exercise and meditation do not diminish over time.

Go for a jog. Sit and breathe. Write words. Repeat.

3 reasons why you need diverse skills to make money as a writer

To become a full-time, professional writer in this day and age, you'll need much more than a deep vocabulary of words at your disposal. It takes a diverse combination of many skills to make your wage month after month.

Here are three reasons why you need diverse skills to make money as a writer.

Reason 1: Choose your income

One of the great things about being a full-time writer is that you get to set and choose your own income. In no way does that mean this will be an easy task. You'll need to send out proposals for new jobs on a daily basis until you win the trust of potential long-term clients. That means that you'll have to manipulate and grow your skill base into new territory based on each project you work on. Do a little article writing? Best to learn SEO marketing. Do a little marketing? Best to learn copy writing.

Reason 2: Not matter what your job is…

Whether you're writing books, articles, screenplays, or a combination of all three, having written fluidity is imperative. This is especially true when having to transcribe projects from MS Word to Final Draft, for example, or vica versa. Having a verbal flexibility, as well as a technological flexibility, will only add to your value as a writer. Which brings us to our next reason why having diverse skills as a writer is important…

Reason 3: Technology

In the age of the internet, full-time writers not only need to be computer savvy, you should make an effort to learn your way around programs such as: HTML, Adobe Creative Cloud, Adobe InDesign, Final Draft, Microsoft Word, Wordpress, Calibre, Sigil, etc. Also, The mechanics of search engine optimization will become your best friend. Know them. In a nutshell, the more technology you master, the better your chances are at landing your next big writing job.

As you can see, learning and mastering a diverse amount of skills is beneficial to your career as a writer in the long-term. As people, we should never stop learning and growing, but as a full-time, professional writer, it is your job.

3 reasons why having a good looking portfolio is so important

Resumes are not only boring, but they are usually not enough to land you those high-paying, sought after jobs. The longevity of your career can often depend on how good of a portfolio you have.

Here are three reasons why having a good looking portfolio is so important and what you can do to build a better one.

Reason 1: Work Experience vs Work Samples

While resumes focus on your previous work history and include useless information such as dates you've worked with companies and your role there, portfolios are a collection of actual work you've done. While this isn't appropriate for *all* types of jobs, for many, it is a much easier way for a potential employer to assess your skills through tangible work would have completed or overseen compared to the often ambiguous job titles and descriptions provided in resumes, which is also why it's important to only put your best work on your portfolio.

Reason 2: Portfolios are a visual presentation of your previous work

Can we all agree that resumes are, overall, pretty boring? They're boring to write as a job seeker and they're boring to read as an employer. Portfolios often provide a better experience for both the employer and employee by presenting a collection of work in a visual manner, as opposed to the text-based presentation of traditional resumes. Not only are portfolios much easier on the eyes, but interactive portfolios actively engage and grab potential employers by breathing some much needed life into stuffy old resumes.

Reason 3: You can build a portfolio just as easy as any resume

There are many websites which allow you to build a visual portfolio featuring samples of your best work for a monthly fee, and a few good free ones, too. It can become quite tedious building the same portfolios on multiple sites, including Coroflot, Behance and Carbonmade.

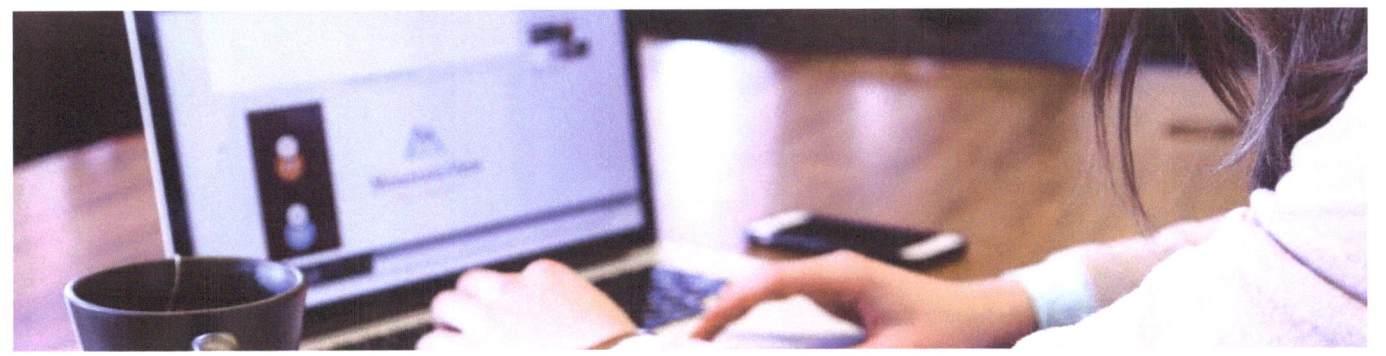

3 Reasons Why having a good looking website is so important

If you don't have your own dedicated website yet, get one. While there are many benefits to having your own website, this article will focus on the top three reasons why getting a website of your own will get you ahead.

Here are three reasons why having a good looking website is so important.

Reason 1: Your employers will notice

If you're serious about your career, having your own website, preferably in your name or on a subject within your niche, definitely adds to your credibility. Rest assure that your client or next employer will certainly take notice of this. Having your portfolio or linking to some of the work you've done is a definite plus. Now you will have something cool to pull up during your next interview!

Reason 2: What's in a name?

When choosing a name for your website, now is not the time to get creative with the domain name. It's best to keep it as simple as your name, some variation of your name, or on a topic within your field or niche. Remember, domain names cannot be changed once you start adding content.

Note that you need both a domain and a host. Know the difference: The domain is the registered web address, such as www.3reasonswhy.com, and the host is the server where all of the data on your website is stored (Hey, it has to go somewhere, right?).

Reason 3: Choose a modest design

What is the best layout or theme for your website? Here is a good rule of thumb: look at the websites for some of the top companies in your field and choose a similar theme.

A Wordpress based site is a very user-friendly blog-type of website with a variety of customizable themes and plug-ins available for free. Do not, however, cheap out and go with a Wordpress or Blogspot subdomain. Again, employers will notice.

3 Reasons Why you should be involved with Speaking, Presenting and Training

There are many benefits involved in public speaking that are not available to those who follow traditional career paths. In fact, according to payscale.com, people who are actively involved in public speaking, presenting, and training make 1.5 times as much annually as those who don't. If that's not reason enough to brush up on your public speaking skills…

Here are three reasons why you should be involved in public speaking, presenting, and training.

Reason 1: You become an expert

In the immortal words of Tim Ferris, "It's much easier to become an expert than you might think." If you have a skill that you've been practicing for a while, ask yourself if you can teach it to other people. Not only is public speaking and training one of the most rewarding parts you'll enjoy later in your career, but in many cases, you become a masterful mentor to those you teach. This newfound status will only prove to help you later in your career.

Congratulation, you are now an expert in your field!

Reason 2: It's a game changer

Your career will only take you to a certain point if you are not partaking in public speaking and training. Once you get involved in public speaking, presenting, and training people within your industry, you'll find that it has a permanent and positive change in your career. You are now seen as a leader with proven managerial capabilities. As history has shown, the only thing that can undo this sort of executive swagger is an embarrassing scandal in the media. Best to stay away from brothels…

Reason 3: Continual Improvement

It's not enough to simply make public appearances and speak to interns about what you know. Great speeches, lectures, and presentations are immortal and can become a part of your legacy. That's why it's important to continually work on improving your presentations. Ask yourself, "Are my thoughts organized as logically as possible? Does this make sense to the listener? Will my listener care about this part?" Tell a story over the course of your presentation to really captivate your audience. Remember to incorporate legitimate statistics or graphs when applicable. And as always, be aware of your body language. Nothing kills a good presentation more than an unconfident public speaker. If you need advice on what a good presentation look like, brush up on your Ted Talks.

As we can see from the reasons listed above, there are many benefits to starting your public speaking, presenting, and training career which you would never normally be able to obtain otherwise.

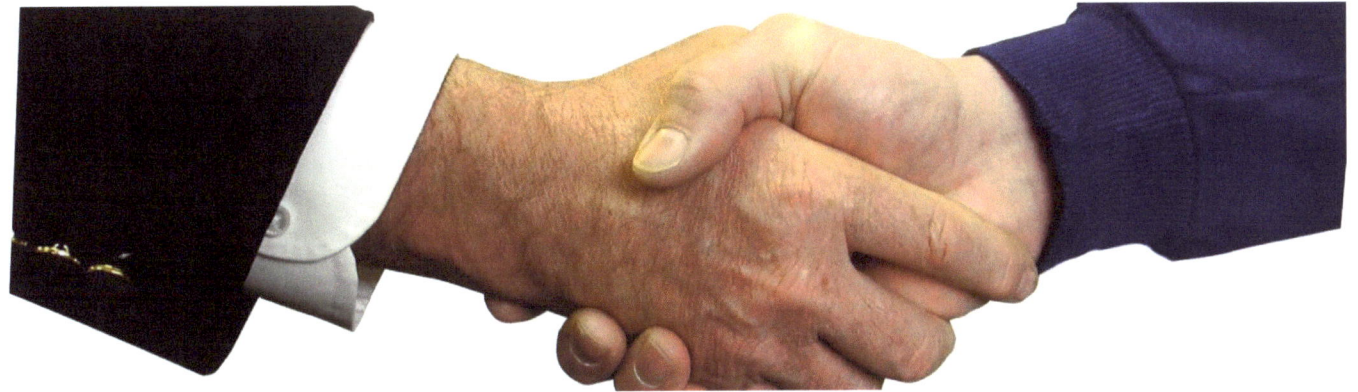

3 Reasons Why networking is your best ally in landing your next job

Although job boards and agencies can be a great source of employment, there is nothing like the limitless potential of networking to find your next job. Proper networking ensure that you have career option to last a lifetime, regardless of what industry you work in, and here's how…

Here are three reasons why networking is your best ally in landing your next job.

Reason 1: It's all about community

If you were to find yourself out of work tomorrow, could you find your next job simply by sending out a few well-written emails or tweets that you are available for work? By building a strong professional network, you can ensure that you are constantly "in high demand", regardless of the state of the economy or your chosen industry. By helping out others within your community, they will want to help you out when that time comes. By doing favors for people within your community, you are able to call in those favors later. With a little work, networking will help you build life-long relationships within your industry.

Reason 2: It's easier than you might think

Networking is not nearly as difficult or intimidating as it may sound. In fact, most networking can be done purely from social media. It can be as simple as promoting yourself within your industry and getting to know other people you work with in the same field. You may already be networking, even if you don't realize it. Any time you go to any outing and talk with friends, neighbors, or strangers about your career, you are networking. You'll find that the longer you do this and the more time you spend in your chosen career, the stronger your network will grow.

Reason 3: It's your best option

In order to land your next job, networking will be your best ally. Don't be afraid to reach out to friends, or even family members while looking for your next job. In fact, the best place to start when you're looking for a new job is to ask around with your network of contacts. Don't be afraid to chat up your acquaintances either. If you work in the same field, chances are that you already have more in common than you think. Sooner than later, you'll be able to turn those acquaintances into good friends and those good friends into potential jobs.

As we can see, landing your next job will be easy when you have built up a strong network. Use the above tips and tactics to help you find your next big gig!

3 Reasons why you need to boost your career by building a personal brand

For many industry professionals, your name is your own personal brand. Even if you work for a larger corporation, if and when you separate from them, you want to be sure that all of the amazing work you've done up until that point follows you for life.

Here are three reasons why you need to boost your career by building a personal brand

Reason 1: What's in a Name?

By using your first and last name in conjunction with your own personal brand, you are rooting yourself in your industry permanently. For this same reason, it's important to introduce yourself with your first and last name. It's not only more memorable, it's more professional as well. It's also important, if you haven't already, to join professional groups related to your industry. While LinkedIn groups are great, professional, paid membership collectives or groups are event better and can only add to your professionalism. Also, it's not enough to just become a passive member of these groups, but you must be an active contributor to their conversation and causes.

Reason 2: Online Presence

The first step to building your personal brand is to establish your online presence. Not only that but, after doing a quick Google search for your name, ask yourself if anything that comes up could possibly be incriminating or come back to haunt you. If you find something embarrassing about yourself on Google's 1st page, you better believe that your potential employers or clients will find it as well. Building a good personal brand is all about establishing a good online presence, so you'll need to replace anything negative you may find about your brand with something positive.

Reason 3: Continual Improvement

One of the most important things to remember while building your personal brand is that you will never stop improving or developing your own brand. Just as you should never stop learning and implementing new ways to develop your own personal brand, you can never stop improving upon your name brand. By doing this, you are effectively engraining yourself into your industry by being able to adapt to any technological changes which may occur.

While there are many benefit and methods to go about building your own personal brand, it all starts with a name. this is your brand and it will follow you for the rest of your life, so why not start improving it today?

3 Reasons Why having mentors pays off big time in your career

Mentors have existed for thousands of years. In many professions throughout history, masters have always taught their apprentices the cornerstones of their trade. The 21st century is no different and the benefits of having a "master" to teach you all of his experience is still as imperative today as it was thousands of years ago.

Here are three reasons why having a mentor pays off big time in your career.

Reason 1: Learn from an Expert

There are many benefits of having a mentor help you throughout the course of your career. By having a mentor teach you're the basics, you are establishing the best possible cornerstone available in your chosen industry – one built on experience. This is, without a doubt, the best way to prepared yourself for a long lasting career with the advice from an "expert" who has already made it. this way, your mentor will be able to teach you all of the ins and outs of the business, in which he or she has already made a name for themselves.

Reason 2: Prepared for the Worst

You will also be able to avoid any of the potential mistakes or failures that they have made in their career. A good mentor will help you prepare for and effectively handle all of the hardships you will inevitably face during the course of your career. By having a mentor, you are better prepared for these speed bumps and hiccups when they inevitably come up. By this method, having a mentor will help you prepare for the worst-case scenarios in your career and avoid pitfalls which you might, under other circumstance, succumb to.

Reason 3: Beyond Mentoring

While mentorships can be effective for any career, they are not the only option for those seeking advice in their industry of choice. Interning can be a great way to learn from a variety of higher-ups in your chosen industry, either by observing or having the opportunity to ask them questions.

College courses are a great way to gain insightful wisdom on any number of courses you may be majoring in, but they lack the real world experience which can only be provided by a mentor. As a cross between college level courses and mentoring, there is a new wave of online training courses becoming widely popular. These video-based, self-paced online training courses involve an industry "expert" teaching you all of his secrets through pre-recorded video tutorials. More importantly, most of these courses come with one or several follow-up calls you can make to the course teacher, which could provide invaluable reflection on the material you just learned.

3 Reasons Why not to get burned-out at the job

The world is a crazy place and it seems like more and more people are finding themselves having to live their lives at breakneck speed just to be able to make it through each day and survive. Given the commercial, technology driven conditions that we now operate in, it is incredibly easy to see why people would very easily find themselves getting burned out. Okay, so obviously no-one consciously wakes up one morning and decides to burn themselves out at work BUT it happens, so, to counter that, here are 3 reasons why not to get burned out at the job:

Reason 1: Your family needs you

We all have families. It doesn't matter whether how those units are made up. Whether it is a spouse and kids that we go home to, or whether we go home to our parents. The key to remember is that family is king and spending some form of quality time with them is a pre-requisite not just to our emotional health but to our physical health too. Yes, you work to pay the bills but it is your family that needs you to remain in one piece.

Reason 2: You have a life to live

Much as it may seem as if your whole life revolves around work, that really doesn't have to be the case. Yes, a lot of people have to work crazy hours. Sometimes they have to work several jobs just to make ends meet. Of course, you have to do whatever it takes. However, if you can focus on something away from the job. Something that drives you forward and spurs you on, then you should find that you don't get so easily burned out.

Reason 3: It's only a job

You may think of it as your career. Your stepping stone to a better life, but at the end of the day while yes you do get to take home a paycheck at the end of each week or each month it is your boss that ultimately benefits from you slaving away for hours on end. Surely, that in itself is reason enough not to allow yourself to get burned out!

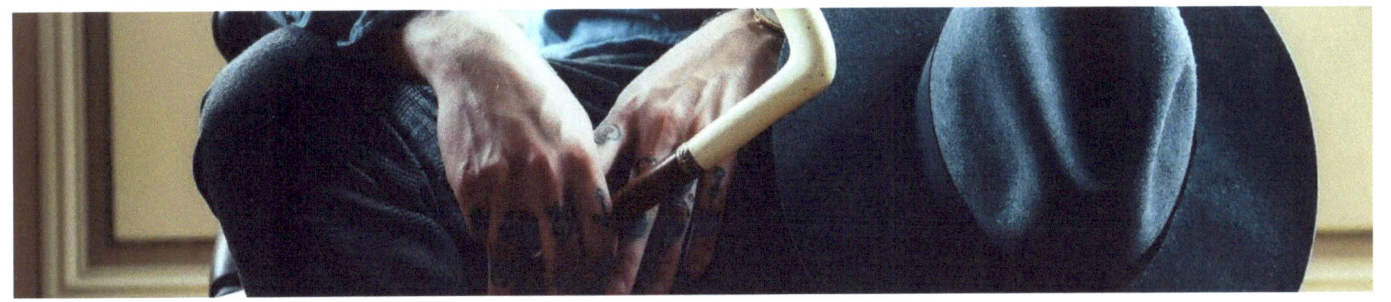

3 Reasons why you are the CEO of your career

In the olden days, the generally prevailing attitude was that most people had to accept their lot in life and get on with it. This meant that those coming from poorer, more disadvantaged backgrounds always got the bum deal and those from more privileged and better off backgrounds got all of the plum jobs. Now, while that system is still in operation in certain quarters, it is becoming less so. There have never been more opportunities for people with a bit of get up and go about them to steam ahead and forge brilliant career paths for themselves.

Here are 3 reasons why you are the CEO of your career.

Reason 1: You are free

Granted, everyone has certain responsibilities that they have to meet; things like bills and childcare. However, the days of slavery are long gone, and while you might not necessarily have the freedom to do everything your own way right now, you are free to take strides in that direction. What does that mean? Well, say you are stuck in a dead end job, what is stopping you from taking a home-study course to gain additional qualifications? Or, applying elsewhere?

Reason 2: No-one says you are not

If you allow society to box you in, then you will find that that you wind up living your whole life in a cage. Really, anything else is just an excuse. You need to learn to start making your own rules of engagement and then living by them. So, next time someone tells you that you have to take a dead end job, or that starting out in your own business is a risky move, tell them to butt out.

Reason 3: Your earning power is in your hands

Once you free yourself from the imaginary constrains you will find that your earning power shoots through the roof. If you want to earn $50k per year, what is stopping you? Chart out a plan and then make it happen.

Far too often we allow ourselves to be pigeon-holed because of the circumstances of our birth. This is really unnecessary! Go live the life you want to live!

3 Reasons Why you must negotiate your salary

It is not all that long ago, that society seemed incredibly rigid when it came to protocols and accepted wisdom as to how people should progress their careers. Thankfully we have moved on a lot from the 1950's and the work place is in general a much more vibrant place not just for women but for workers everywhere. So, with the changing times come changing attitudes. Do you have to accept your lot in life? Do you have to accept the pay packet and salary that your boss offers you? No, absolutely not!

Here are 3 reasons why you MUST negotiate your salary.

Reason 1: Employers will pay as little as possible

This all comes down to business sense and savvy really. No employer in their right mind is going to pay out a salary of $30k p.a. if they can get away with paying $20k. Negotiating your salary is not just for high-earners. Anyone, regardless of their entry level, can with a little confidence negotiate. Okay, so you might not be going in there and demanding huge salary increases, but there is no harm in at least trying to make the terms and conditions more favorable to you!

Reason 2: If you don't value yourself how can you expect others to?

There is an awful lot of sense in this. You owe it to yourself to earn as much as you possibly can. Yes, of course, you have to keep it real. A barista is never going to earn a salary of $50k per year. However, there is no reason why you can't get a better deal. Just think about what even an extra $400 dollars would get you?

Reason 3: You will earn more respect

Someone with the nous and guts to negotiate their salary is likely to be more confident and the conventional wisdom is that they will bring more value to the party than someone who just sits back and lets life happen to them. Even if you don't earn yourself the extra pay rise, your employer is far less likely to take you for granted.

There are dozens of other reasons why it is incredibly important that you do whatever you can to negotiate your salary. Hopefully this brief article will have given you some food for thought.

3 Reasons Why you should believe in the 'Fake It Til You Make It' mantra

Everyone knows someone who flounces around as if they are the bees-knees, lording it up over everyone. While we all know that most of these people are all fur coat and no knickers, there is also a tiny part of us that wonders if maybe they really are living the high life. If they are utterly loaded. That is the crux of the matter. While some people will most definitely argue that this tactic is incredibly shallow and tacky there is a whole army of people across the world that wholeheartedly subscribes to it.

Here are three reasons why you should believe in the Fake it until you make it mantra.

The laws of attraction

While this is not scientifically proven, there is a strong argument that people who think positive and behave in a certain way have a tendency to attract that kind of lifestyle. So, by living and breathing the Fake it Till you Make it mantra you are turning it into a self-fulfilling prophecy. Whether or not you believe in the universal laws of attraction or not, this should definitely provide food for thought.

It could actually happen

As far as strategies go, this one is definitely better than pinning all of your hopes on winning the lottery. By faking it, you could easily wind up making your way into a luxurious lifestyle that would not have been possible if people believed that you lived in some skanky apartment in Queens. There is more merit in this strategy than people give it credit for.

The feel good factor

Don't ever underestimate the power of the feel good factor! Put it another way, if you spend your life thinking that you are doomed to a life of drudgery, where nothing good will happen, well, it kind of gets to the point where you question the point. On the flip side by believing in the fake it till you make it mantra you get to have some awesome experiences.

This mantra is definitely not for everyone. However, if it is not hurting anyone then what's the problem with it. Live and let live!

3 Reasons why you must learn to hold yourself accountable

If you were to conduct a random straw poll of say one-hundred people, what are the chances that a high percentage of them will be able to reel off countless occasions where someone has given them bad customer service, or they have felt let down by the fact that someone hasn't taken responsibility for their actions? Lack of accountability is disappointingly commonplace in the modern day world. Maybe it is a dying trait; one more frequently found in the older generations, or maybe it is down to a simple lack of manners. However, here are 3 reasons why you must learn to hold yourself accountable.

Reason 1: It is an essential life skill

Okay, while yes, some people seem to do rather well out of life by doing the exact opposite and not taking responsibility for their actions and words if you want to be liked and respected by your peers then this really is an essential life skill. You have to be willing to clean up your own mess, in the same way as if you make a promise or a commitment to do something, then you should do your utmost to see it through. Deadlines are kind of like that too!

Reason 2: It will increase your chances of a better career

After reliability then the next thing that a lot of employers look for in their staff is accountability. If someone is going through the trouble of hiring you then they need to be pretty certain that if you screw up then you will be man enough to fix things. People who can demonstrate that they have a handle on this, often find themselves being fast tracked up the corporate career ladder.

Reason 3: Your children need to see this in you

One of the main reasons why our society is in the mess that it is in because not enough parents demonstrate the power of accountability to their kids. As a parent, one of the greatest gifts that you can give your child is letting them see that you are humble enough to own up to your mistakes and then attempt to fix it.

Accountability truly can't be underestimated. Just imagine if the shoe were on the other foot and someone else had made a mistake. You would expect them to put it right, correct?

3 Reasons why salary alone is not the only metric for good compensation

If you were to ask the majority of people why they go to work most would look at you as though you had lost your marbles and reply that they go to work to earn money. Fair point. However, do any of those people ever stop and think about whether or not money is the only measure for whether or not they are being fairly compensated in the work place. The reality is that more and more people are looking for something extra.

Here are three reasons why salary alone is not the only metric for good compensation:

Reason 1: Work life balance

Everyone needs cash in which to pay their bills; things like their mortgage and to put food on the table each day. However, as the old saying goes money doesn't buy you everything, and once you have addressed the basics then you have to start questioning whether your job enables you to have a decent work life balance. Again, this is incredibly subjective. We don't all share the same ideas as to what constitutes work life balance. For some, it might mean spending time with their families. For others it might mean having enough time to escape and go hiking for the weekend.

Reason 2: Can you take time off in a crisis?

It's all very well and good getting paid $80k per year. However, what use is that if it means that the price you pay is missing your daughter's wedding, or are not able to make it to the hospital in time to say goodbye to a parent? Many enlightened people would gladly take a small cut in salary if it meant that that had greater flexibility in which to deal with life's crises.

Reason 3: Is it harmful to your health?

This is not as stupid is at sounds. Yes, most people would think that most jobs in the twenty-first century in modern day America would be fully health and safety compliant. However, the sad fact is that they are not always. Is it really worth sacrificing your health over a job. Meaning your mental health as well as your physical health. There are so many stress-related deaths each year, that maybe people need to start factoring this into the equation.

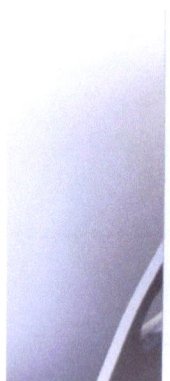

3 Reasons Why resumes alone can be boring for your career

Conventional wisdom dictates that resumes are essential for procuring work and furthering one's career. If fact, this is drummed into students from a very early age. Way before they are ever ready to even go and get a part time Saturday job! Because most people that you know will have prepared a resume at least once in their lives, then it is expected that this is the way that you do things. This is actually a very dangerous concept. It is too blinkered.

Here are 3 reasons why resumes alone can be boring for your career:

Reason 1: They don't give an accurate picture

While resumes offer a concise and provided you have been truthful, honest account of a person's career and accomplishments to date, they very rarely, if indeed ever reveal anything about their actual personality. What makes them tick? Who they are. Resumes are bland by nature and have been designed to stifle personality.

Reason 2: They don't enable any engagement

Here's how the process goes. You type up your resume. You send it off to a number of potential employers who flick through it, and on the basis of what you have provided decide whether or not they are going to invite you in for an interview. During the interview they may or may not refer to the resume as a point of reference. At no point during this process, yes – even the interview process, do they allow for any engagement, which is very boring.

Reason 3: They don't allow you to showcase your creativity

Resumes are very formulaic, they are nothing more than templates, designed by someone zillions of years ago before the internet who figured that businesses required uniformity and consistency. The lack of creativity is very uninspiring, and yes, boring.

So, now that you know why a resume isn't the be all and end all, maybe it is time to start thinking just what you can do to make the situation better.

The 3 Reasons Why Book of Money & Business

3 Reasons why Not All companies contribute equally to your career

You'd be amazed at just how many people trundle through life without giving any thought as to just exactly what the company that they are presently working for is doing for them or their career. There is a widely held belief that you go to work, do the best that you can but ultimately that you should be simply grateful for the fact that you are in employment. The notion that an employer can somehow contribute to your career is regarded by many as purely fantastical. Now that you have begun to think about it though, maybe you would like to know a three reasons why not all companies contribute equally to your career:

Reason 1: You don't expect them to

Yes, this point has already been made. However, it is a fact that they reason why not all companies contribute to your career is that you don't expect them to. By being passive, you are effectively handing control of your career over to them. By re-wiring your expectations you should see some incredible results.

Reason 2: Some employers aren't employee focused.

It is a sad fact of life that not all employers are focused on their employees. Indeed, many just see them as a cog in the wheel. If that sound Dickensian to you, take a look around you. Do a little research and you will see that it is not too wide of the mark! Until employees start challenging unacceptable practices and demanding more parity across the board then unfortunately precious little is going to change.

Reason 3: They might not know how

While there are definitely some rotten eggs out there, many employers do still want to do the right thing by their employees. They recognize that by looking after their staff they will reduce their turnover, which in turn reduces the amount of money that they need to invest on training and recruitment. A company that knows how to retain its staff is usually a profitable one. If you are unhappy, tell your boss and see if you can come up with an effective strategy between the two of you.

3 Reasons why being a generalist wins you the world

The politically correct world that we live in today has thrown up oodles of new terminologies and phrases which are now widely in circulation in society. However, in layman's terms a generalist is simply a good, all-rounder. Someone that is generally competent in various different walks of life, or things that they do. Had that eureka moment yet?

Here are 3 reasons why being a generalist will win you the world.

Reason 1: They have greater flexibility

If someone only has a particular skillset that they are not able to expand upon or take into other areas of their life, no matter how skilled or specialist they may be in their given field they are not going to have the same potential as some that is say a little less skilled but can cover a much broader remit.

Reason 2: If something doesn't work out they can quickly move on

Let's face it, most people have found themselves in that horrid situation where the job they are working doesn't seem to be leading anywhere, or the relationship that they are in doesn't seem to be working out. A generalist wouldn't worry about such minutia. They would simply move onto something or someone else. Okay, so putting relationships in this category is a little blunt, but it is truthful.

Reason 3: They will be less risk averse.

Learning new skills is notoriously challenging. If someone doesn't like to be taken out of their comfort zone, then they are going to find even taking a new online course traumatic. A generalist on the other hand, because they are great at multi-tasking should find this an absolute doddle. Okay, so sometimes we do need to be risk aware, but there is a world of difference between this and being risk averse.

People, who can wear several different hats, who are maybe moderately good at several different things rather than being fantastic at one thing are far more likely to live their dream.

3 Reasons Why your primary goal should be to add value to others

You can choose all of the right strategies to market yourself, but at the end of the day, you will remain unsuccessful in your career if you don't actively add value to others. This often happens when you are focused on yourself and your own goals. While there is nothing wrong with being career-focused, your selfishness will be plain-as-day to other people and you may miss out on important networking opportunities as a result.

Many people look at their career and want to be the top dog. If you're the type of person who gets jealous when seeing someone else in the same industry as you succeed instead of congratulating them and being happy for them - or worse - the type who actively sabotages other people's careers, then don't be surprised when your career doesn't go anywhere. True success is measured by the value that you provide to other people.

Here are three reasons why your primary goal should be to add value to others.

Reason 1: Favors are often reciprocated

While your goal should be to help others just for the sake of helping others, when youdo a favor for someone, they will feel obligated to repay you in kind. Little favors make the world go 'round, which is true in every career. You cannot "buy" favors from people, but by adding value to other people, they will be more inclined to add value to you in the future.

Reason 2: It makes you look good

If you're not adding value to other people just to make them look good, think about how helping out other people will make you look in the eyes of other people in your industry. This is an age old secret to success: by investing in other people, you are making an investment in yourself. When other influences in your industry see you selflessly doing good deeds, they will be more incline to help you. Call it karma if you want, but good things inevitably happen to people who help other people.

Reason 3: It's the nice thing to do

If a buddy calls you up at 3 a.m. and tells you tyhat he is stranded and needs a ride, what will you do? Any good friend would come to his rescue. Not only will your buddy be more inclined to do a favor for you in the future, but it's the right thing to do by helping someone out in need; so should it be in your career.

3 Reasons Why having a routine can do wonders for your career

In every business, there is a very precise and organized system in place which is perfectly structured in order to achieve certain results on a daily basis. Every successful business in every industry is structured by a daily routine, so, too, should your daily life in order to achieve success with your career.

Here are three reasons why having a routine can do wonders for your career.

Reason 1: Biological alarm clock.

Keeping to your daily routine will ensure that your body grows accustomed to every aspect of your career. That means that if you need to be in the office at 6 a.m. every day, but you plan on sitting in traffic for 30 minutes, you need to set your alarm clock for 5 a.m. That will give you 30 minutes to eat, dress, shower and hit the road in order to make it to the office in time. If this is a new job, then the first few weeks of waking up at 5 a.m. to a loud, buzzing alarm clock might be rough for you. The following month, however, you may find yourself waking up a few minutes before the alarm clock sounds. Because you have forced your body into a daily routine, you can now enjoy the benefits of an internal, or biological, alarm clock. Now, good luck sleeping in on the weekend!

Reason 2: It's a time-saver.

After you get into a routine that you follow every day, you'll find that tasks which used to be difficult are now easy and tasks which used to take a long time are now completed in no time at all. Chock this one up to "practice makes perfect". You may have never thought about wanting to become a master of sending those annoying-yes-essential emails, filing those weekly reports, and yes, even doing your laundry at the same time every week will make our life that much easier once you simply get into the routine of doing it.

Reason 3: It relieves stress at work.

You know that little sigh of relief you breathe every time you check an item off of your "to-do" list? Having a routine is a lot like that, only you're constantly checking items off of your list all day, one after another, and they are all super easy because you are in the routine of completing them. One little success begets another and so forth.

3 Reasons Why it takes grit to work remotely

Everyone loves the idea of working remotely, but is it really all it's cracked up to be? Here are three reasons why it takes grit to work remotely.

Reason 1: You Lose Focus

Working remotely is the same thing as working at home, but environment of your house is not the same as that of the office. There are a lot of distractions everywhere you turn while working at home which can prevent getting into that state of comfortable work flow. Simple things like the television, laundry and dirty dishes piling up can easily distract from getting real work done. Most people that work remotely try to get through the day by multitasking chores around the house with their actual work, which lowers their overall productivity and quality of work.

Reason 2: You lose boundaries

While your friends and family understand that, when you work in an office, you cannot answer their calls or messages. A lot of people see working from home as having the freedom to do whatever you want, which it is to a certain extent. Just because you work from home isn't going to stop your friends and family members from dropping in unannounced or sending you text messages all day. When you work remotely, it is even more important to draw the boundaries that separate your work time from your leisure time – and it's equally important to make sure that other people know the difference, too!

Reason 3: You become isolated

It takes a great courage to work from home all by yourself. In the office, there are colleagues who you chat with, you can go out for lunch together and so on. When you're working remotely, on the other hand, the is very limited human interaction at all, save for a few Skype chats with clients here and there. When working remotely, it is vital that you get at least 30 minutes of authentic human interaction each day. Sure, you have things like Facebook and Twitter, but social media is no supplement for a one-on-one conversation with another person. It may sound funny, but if you go months at a time without interfacing with another human being, you'll be surprised how quickly your social skills will deteriorate.

ENTREPRENEURSHIP

3 Reasons why perfection is not a prerequisite for success

Perfection is hard. It's so hard, in fact, that it might not even exist. In the minds of creative people who keep chasing the elusive state of "perfection", done is often never good enough. However, perfection is definitely not a prerequisite for success, as we'll see…

Here are three reasons why perfection is not a prerequisite for success.

Reason 1: Done is often better than perfect

The words, "The most beautiful diamond in the world is worthless if you don't show it to anyone." Have always stuck with me. Especially true for creative individuals and producers, we may often think that our final product is not good enough to put out into the world. Once released into the world, if the response is overwhelmingly negative, then we can easily pull it back, tweak it to perfection, and give it a second chance. There are often no mistakes than cannot be undone this way and no permanent damage done.

Reason 2: Timeliness

As an old adage goes, "The minute a printed directory hits the streets, it's out of date." Which is even true in the age of Google. How many times have you been on Google Maps, looking for a place, only to find out that it no longer exists? If we hold on to the content we have, trying to tweak and perfect it in any way we can, sooner or later the next big thing is going to come along and render all of our hard work useless. Do yourself a favor and release it as soon as it's done rather than when you feel it is "perfect".

Reason 3: There is no such thing as perfect

Create people who producing physical, tangent things often feel that their work is never complete or perfect. It can always be improved, and this sentiment is only holding us back! Life is about success, not perfection, which is illustrated by other successful people. What if Ford had never built the assembly line because he was nervous about what other people would think about it? do yourself a favor and release whatever you've made out into the world before it becomes outdated – it's the only true way to become successful!

As we can see from the three reasons listed here, perfection is definitely not a prerequisite for success. it might be difficult for the perfectionists in all of us, but it is often easier to release something out into the world when it is complete rather than perfect.

3 Reasons why your dreams must be intimidating to you to ensure great success in life

Falling out of an airplane with a parachute – definitely intimidating. Giving a speech to a crowd of 100,000 people, also intimidating. But which one will bring us success in life and which one is fantasy? I should hope that you answer the latter. In fact, your dreams need to be intimidating in order for us to succeed in life.

Here are three reasons why your dreams must be intimidating to ensure your success in life.

Reason 1: Setting big goals

We all know about the importance of setting big goals for ourselves. Having one or several big goals at the top of a longer list of small goals gives us something to look forward to every day. This is why it's important to dream big, even if that dream is initially intimidating, while we work towards that big goal every day. As we slowly close the distance, that big, intimidating dream will seem less intimidating as we close in on it. success if surely within all of our grasps, and no dream is too intimidating to achieve with the proper set of goals and work ethic.

Reason 2: Setting smaller goals

On the path to your big goal should be an equally intimidating, but doable, list of smaller goals to help you reach the biggest one. With these smaller goals, it is important that they will help you achieve the large goal over time. Write down the small goals and a timeline by which you hope to achieve them, then stick to it. A research study found that people who wrote down their physical goals and a due date for all of them achieved 90% more than those who did not. Whether you're good with deadlines or not, knowing your direction is half of dreaming big and meeting your goals.

Reason 3: Dream big or go home!

No one ever gained anything by setting small goals and dreaming small dreams. If you don't set high, lofty goals for yourself, you have nowhere to climb to! By setting the biggest goals possible, we guarantee at least some level of success, for "even if I aim for the moon and miss, at least I will be among the stars."

As we can see from the above reasons, you must set big goals for yourself, along with an equally intimidating list of smaller goals leading up to the big ones, in order to be successful. If you don't dream big, you don't win big. So next time you're having a bit of introspection, try thinking – and dreaming – as big as possible.

3 Reasons why you need ambassadors for you brand

You may be wondering why many companies seem to get ahead much quicker than other, similar companies. Here are three reasons why you need an ambassador for your brand.

Reason 1: Corporate Identity

By having an individual as a brand ambassador, you are basically telling customers, "Hey, we're not some faceless corporation just trying to make a buck. We're real people, too!" A sense of corporate identity is important with customers. By humanizing your brand, your effective lift the reputation of your entire brand in the eyes of your customers. This will become very important in the long run and it's best to establish one or several brand ambassadors early on in your company's history.

Reason 2: Marketing

A good brand ambassador will put your company or product on the map without even trying. Brand ambassadors provide your brand with the visibility that it wouldn't normally be able to get. An effective brand ambassador could be as simple as being someone who is not affiliated with the company, although is credible and respected within the company's field, sending out posts on various social networks in support of your brand. By this means, a good brand ambassador will also help to expand your company's social reach. Use brand ambassadors in different regions to help expand your company worldwide!

Reason 3: Customer Service

Strategic use of brand ambassadors will not only help to promote and market your products, but will also help customer service by actively protecting your brand's reputation. If your brand ambassador already has a strong professional network within the same industry as your company, they are passively doing the footwork of building your brand's reputation and customer service. By properly implementing your brand's ambassador, you are also able to quickly and effectively address bad reviews of your product or service and undo potentially negative effects.

The great thing about having a brand ambassador is that it could be anyone. From several members of the press to a paid professional who does exclusive marketing for your company, brand ambassadors can be just about anyone and

The use of multiple brand ambassadors, when used effectively, will establish a corporate identity for your brand, promote and market your brand and passively produce positive customer service while addressing negative reviews.

3 Reasons Why the TV show Shark Tank is such a hit around the world

Reality TV shows are so popular nowadays. They're making waves in the entertainment industry as they become the most in-demand shows on television. The brainchild of Sony Pictures TV with Mark Burnett as its executive producer, Shark Tank is a reality TV show of a different variety. The show features would-be entrepreneurs who have the opportunity to pitch their business ideas to the "sharks" or major investors. But why did America fall in love with ABC's sharks?

Here are three reasons why the TV show Shark Tank is such a hit around the world.

Reason 1: The chance to chase the American dream.

With the television air waves oversaturated with reality TV shows, none are more exciting and life-changing than Shark Tank. That's because the lucky contestants who get to enter the Tank and pitch their business ideas to the Sharks are given the chance to chase the American dream and succeed in their chosen venture. The Sharks are successful millionaires who are more than willing to finance business ideas in order to fill their own pockets by investing.

Reason 2: It's completely unscripted.

You never know what's going to happen in the Tank! Shark Tank is unscripted, which is one of the reasons it's so appealing to viewers. There's drama, action, suspense, and comedy in each episode, and the actors are real people who're not told what to do or say. They're free to express themselves, so audience sees all of their excitement as well as their forlornness when the Sharks eat 'em up. Another priceless Shark Tank moment you won't find anywhere else on TV is when the investors fight one another in order to get a piece of the same investment.

Reason 3: Award-winning TV show.

Shark Tank is not just there to entertain viewers. It is a multi-awarded reality show with millions of fans around the world. The show recently garnered the Outstanding Structured Reality Program at the Emmy's for the second year in a row and was nominated for Outstanding Picture Editing for Reality Programming. In 2014 it was nominated for Outstanding Directing for Nonfiction Programming also at the Emmy's.

Shark Tank TV show is such a big hit around the world, and for good reason. It is a life-changing series that give opportunities for aspiring entrepreneurs and, unlike with other shows on television, it is unscripted and has garnered several awards.

3 Reasons why people skills are key

All of us know those gregarious individuals who are always the life of the party, and the office. But what makes them so special, and just how far can having great people skills take you in life?

Here are three reasons why people skills are key.

Reason 1: Communication

Having great communication skills will take you very far in life. They are the basis on which all careers are built. But having an above average level of communication will not only help you to succeed in your career, it is also the key to having, and keeping, healthy relationships. Communication begins with clarity and honesty. This is best done conversationally by providing thoughtful responses rather than rapid-fire responses. Also important to communication is the ability to match the mood and tone of the person to whom you are speaking. By staying focused and calm during conversation, your communication skills will increase and, as a result, your people skills.

Also important to communication is our comprehension of non-verbal cues and predicting or anticipate social situations before they occur.

Reason 2: Networking

It's no secret that networking is one of the keys to success, and people skills are a huge part, if not the only part, of networking. A huge part of networking, of course, is empathy and putting yourself in the shoes of the person with whom you are speaking. Having a high-functioning emotional intelligence plays a very important part in networking. Additionally, good self-management is one of the pillars of emotional intelligence and absolutely fundamental for leadership success.

Reason 3: Great Conversation

The untold, primary benefit of having great people skills is plain old great conversation. This starts with having enough comprehension of the situation to as great questions, which is an art form in itself. Great conversations first arise from environmental assessment and social awareness, all of which contribute to having great people skills.

Finally, good manners are what brings together all of our people skills in a way which makes them flow naturally. Obviously, some of these factors which are attributed to good people skills may come more naturally to some than others, but with a little practice, anyone can be mixing and mingling with the best.

3 Reasons why you must teach yourself how to learn

Most people never stop learning or growing. While the constant uptake of new information is imperative to all of our lives, in order to become successful in life, learning is an even more important skill.

Here are three reasons why you must teach yourself to learn

Reason 1: Learning always has been and always will be the key to success

Take a look at all of the most successful people of today. What do they all have in common? Every successful person is an exceptionally fast learner. Not only that, buy the key to success lies in one's willingness to adapt. To take it one step further, successful individuals have an inherent desire to learn new things and are always seeking out new information.

Reason 2: Learn your preferred method of learning

We all have a preferred method of learning. Are you able to pick-up information simply by listening to a lecture, or do you need a more visual aspect? Would you learn better if you wrote everything down? It's best to find out your preferred method of learning as early as possible, however, contrary to the old adage: old dogs can always learn new tricks.

Reason 3: Beyond trial and error

It's often said that a smart man learns from his mistakes, but a wise man learned from the mistake of others. This is why learning about history, especial that of other companies within your chosen field, is so important.

Alternatively, there is always the option of finding someone to teach you. Having a mentor is very important when pursuing any endeavor in life, however, learning quickly is still a huge part of having a mentor or teacher. With someone teaching you the specific things which you are trying to learn, you may become more successful much quicker. When we have an inherent interest in that which we are learning, the rate of learned information grows exponentially.

3 Reasons Why cultivating a daily writing habit is important

Writing is a part of everyday life, which is why it's vital that you learn to cultivate it. It is a skill that needs to be developed from a young age. Many people find writing beneficial because it makes them better communicators while some are also earning a lot of money from it.

Here are the reasons why cultivating a daily writing habit is important.

Reason 1: Improve your writing skills

Establishing a daily writing habit can greatly improve your writing skills. You don't have to spend the whole day writing, because it only requires about fifteen minutes of your time every day. What's important is you devote time to it daily to establish a routine or schedule. Consider this as a form of practice. You can never improve your skills if you only write whenever you feel like it. To be successful, you have to make writing a habit you can't live without.

Reason 2: To express yourself

People have different ways of expressing themselves. There are those who can pretty much express their thoughts and emotions through singing or dancing, while some turn to writing. Many individuals have diaries where they used to write everything and in today's digital world there's social media and blogging. You can write about anything and later reflect on it. Reading what you have written can help you find answers to what went wrong or right in your life and how to improve yourself and your future.

Reason 3: Earn money

How would you like to be your own boss and earn more than enough? Consider being a writer and earning money doing what you love the most. But not all writers are born talented: some have to develop their skill. This is where a daily writing habit comes in. You don't have to do it in your bedroom or office, you can write anywhere. J.K. Rowling, famous author of the Harry Potter series, said that you should write in whatever time you have.

Whether you want a career in writing or simply want to enhance your writing skills, cultivating a daily writing habit is important. It will greatly improve your skills as a writer, allow you to express yourself, and possibly help you earn some money.

3 Reasons why not to take yourself too seriously sometimes

Everyone has bouts when they just cannot see the funny side of life regardless of how funny or crazy a situation may seem. However, taking yourself too seriously can seriously impact on so many areas of your life, and can lead to some terrible misunderstandings. No-one wants to be seen as that anal guy from down the road, do they?

Here are 3 reasons why you should not take yourself too seriously sometimes:

Reason 1: You will lose friends

No-one wants to be with that person that just cannot wind down, or loosen up. Or that person who people perceives to be full of themselves. Most people need to have a laugh from time to time. They want to be able to relax when they are in your company. Not only do people who take themselves too seriously frequently lose friends but they also find it difficult to make friends in the first place. Don't put yourself in that situation!

Reason 2: You might suffer issues with self-esteem

Because people will frequently misunderstand your intentions if you seem stuck up, then this might then lead to issues with your self-confidence and self- esteem. All of which can lead to a whole host of complex social issues. Lighten up, you will feel better for it!

Reason 3: You could suffer at work or in class

People who take themselves too seriously, frequently find themselves the butt of other people's jokes either in class or at work. This is a terrible situation to find yourself in and can be incredibly isolating. It can also seriously damage your career and promotion prospects.

There are million other reasons why you should lighten up and go with the flow. If this has been a problem for you up until now, then it is never too late to re-evaluate your behavior.

3 Reasons Why you should honor your word

As children, people were already taught by their parents to honor their word. This means sticking to what you have promised or said no matter what happens. However, many still fail when it comes to honoring their word, especially today when it's so easy to make promises and share your thoughts and never have to stick to them in the end.

Here are three reasons why you should honor your word.

Reason 1: To gain trust

Trust is the basic foundation of all relationships. Without it, a relationship will never ever work. Honoring your word is very important because it is one effective way to gain other people's trust. You can never be able to prove yourself as someone trustworthy unless you have taken time to prove it to them. Honoring your word is the simplest and easiest way to prove to someone that you are indeed a person worthy of their trust.

Reason 2: To gain respect

Did you know that people who can be trusted are also highly respected? Honoring your word is a sign to others that you're not only trustworthy, but someone who is also worthy of respect. People will admire you for your remarkable character and will even strive to follow in your footsteps. If you're a parent who shows your children that you honor your word, you will become an admirable role model to them and, with a little luck, it will rub off.

Reason 3: To prove you're a professional

Another reason why you should honor your word is because you are a professional. You're a learned individual who was brought up correctly by your parents. As a professional, you show everybody that you can make promises and never break them. You are very careful with the words that come out of your mouth, too, and never promise something you know you can't do in the first place.

You should learn to honor your word because it is one way to gain the trust of people around you. It's also an excellent way to gain their respect. Further, bear in mind that honoring your word is a sign that you're a professional.

3 Reasons Why Walking away isn't losing

When people walk away from a situation, it doesn't always mean that they lose. People may walk away after losing in a competition, being hurt by someone they love, failing in garnering their prospects, and other similar circumstances. It's not losing at all, though, because sometimes walking away is the smartest move you'll ever make.

Here are the reasons why walking away isn't losing.

Reason 1: Avoid humiliation

Obviously, people walk away after losing to avoid humiliation. For example, if you're turned down by a girl you like, instead of insisting that she goes out with you, you just walk away so you don't get your pride totally burned. When it comes to business, it's also smarter to just excuse yourself and walk away rather than listening to an agent talk about products and services you're not interested in. You'll be saving yourself the trouble, but also the agent from being humiliated.

Reason 2: Respect for others

There are many situations where walking away is the most respectful thing you can do to others. Take for instance when you're in a competition and you lost. As a sign of respect, you just walk away after saying your congratulations to the winner instead of staying and saying bad things against your competitors and the judges. This is also true when you're marketing a product or service. Learn to walk away from your prospective customers who are obviously not interested.

Reason 3: Avoid conflict

In relationships, it's normal to be in conflict from time to time because it's part of growth. A good example is when you and your partner disagree or fight about something. Instead of biting each other's heads off, just be humble and walk away. You can clear your head and think better afterwards. This is also applicable when there's conflict in the workplace. One should learn to be humble and swallow his or her pride for the benefit of the group.

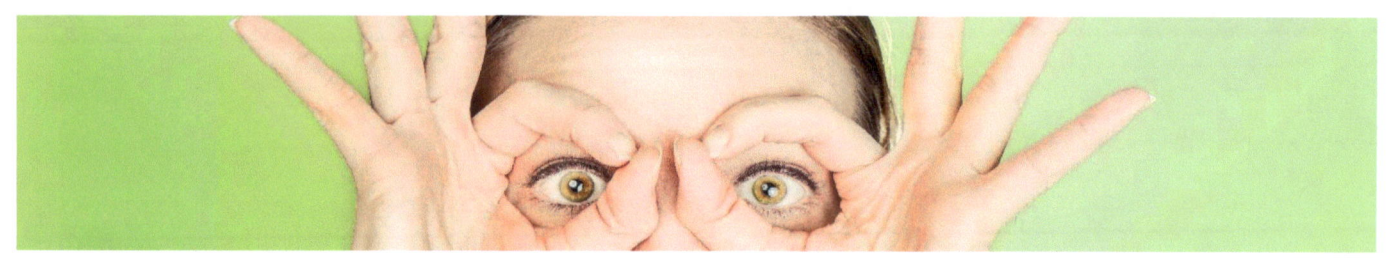

3 Reasons Why Your attitude influences results

Attitude is the solid foundation which sustains successful individuals. It can be our best friend or our worst enemy. It is something we possess which can draw or repel others. One thing you should know is that your attitude is controllable by you, and not by your environment or others.

Here are the reasons why your attitude influences results.

Reason 1: Attitude affects performance

Did you know that your performance at work is affected by the kind of attitude you possess? For instance, if you were given a task with a very strict deadline, how would you react to it? Pessimists would immediately complain and utter excuses not to take the job at all. This kind of attitude is unfavorable in the workplace. The best attitude is to take the task and try your best to finish it on time. Be positive that even though it's a very challenging task, you can still do it. You'll be rewarded for your positive work attitude.

Reason 2: Attitude affects relationships

When we talk about relationships, it's not only about you and your partner, but how you deal with other people around you as well. Attitude can greatly affect your relationship with other individuals. For example, if they see you as someone who is friendly, approachable, respectful, and loyal, chances are you'll gain many more friends than others who don't possess good attitudes. You also learn to deal with other people responsibly and to patch up problems as soon as they arise.

Reason 3: Attitude affects one's outlook in life

People are the ones responsible for the kind of life they have. If you have a negative outlook towards life, then you'll never succeed as a person or professional. Having the right attitude allows one to conquer life's many obstacles. People all face trials, but it's how they deal with them that matters the most. Always look at the brighter side of things and bear in mind that everything happens for a reason.

The kind of attitude you have has a great impact on how successful you'll become in the future. It also defines you as a person. It influences results because it affects your performance, relationship with other people, and also your outlook in life.

The 3 Reasons Why Book of Money & Business

3 Reasons Why Being Hungry keeps you motivated

If you've seen *Hunger Games*, then you know by now why there are people who are motivated to do something because of hunger. It's no wonder that there are those who really aspire to get out of poverty and the hunger they've experienced as a child or adults serves as a motivation to them to do better in life.

Here are the reasons why being hungry keeps you motivated.

Reason 1: Inspires you to work harder

Without money you can never buy anything, including your basic needs such as food and shelter. This is one reason why hunger can motivate people, especially the poor. They take on multiple jobs to earn enough to feed themselves and their families. They often work overtime just so they can earn more. Indeed, hunger is an inspiration for one to work harder.

Reason 2: Motivates you to work faster

The body needs food to keep going, however there are times when you need to finish something important like meeting a very tight deadline. Even though your stomach is already growling in hunger, you have to finish the task or else it will cost you your job. In instances like this, hungers serve as your motivation to work faster. You want everything done on time and also to prevent yourself from starving to death.

Reason 3: Challenge you to do more

People who've experienced what it was like to live in a house wherein they can barely eat three meals a day will find hunger as a challenge for them to do more. They need to earn enough money to buy food and because of this they decide to have more than one job or earn extra by working on weekends or during long breaks. Their empty stomachs are a reminder that they have to do more to eat more.

3 Reasons Why We should learn to forgive, no matter what

Forgiving a person who did you wrong can be very difficult and even painful, especially if damage was already done. But as humans, it's imperative that we learn to forgive, no matter what.

Here are the reasons why we should learn to forgive, no matter what.

Reason 1: It's the right thing to do

Don't worry about what other people do or say and focus on yourself. Know that nothing in this world is so devastating to be considered unforgivable. It's the right thing to do.

Reason 2: To avoid the past from destroying your future

You can never move on from a bad and painful experience if you never forgive those who sinned against you in the first place. The memories will constantly haunt you and plant a seed of hate in your heart which will continue to grow for years. The best thing to do is to forgive, even if the person who did you wrong didn't say sorry for you to have peace of mind. Forgive him or her anyway because it is the only way for you to focus on a brighter future.

Reason 3: Forgive and you'll be forgiven

Remember the golden rule and apply it even in forgiveness. If you forgive others for their wrongs, you, too, will be forgiven. It's like a give and take process everybody will benefit from. People are not perfect, everybody makes mistakes. What's important is you learn from these mistakes and admit you're wrong.

Learning to forgive no matter what is important if you want to live a happy life. Forgive those who sin against you because it's morally correct to do so. It is also one way to prevent your past from destroying what you have ahead of you. Most importantly, you'll also be forgiven for your sins if you forgive others.

3 Reasons why your brain alone is not enough and you need a personal wiki

There can be no disputing the fact that the world in which we live today is grueling, arduous and relentless. You have two choices. You can either keep harking back to the "Good old days" when everything was so much easier, or you can move with the times and get ahead of the game. The reality is that when you have to juggle family responsibilities with work commitments and a million other things you cannot rely on your memory alone to get you through life. This is NOT an admission of failure, nor is a sign that you are prone to senior moments. It is simply a reality of life.

Here are 3 reasons why your brain alone is not enough and you need a personal wiki.

Reason 1: It is multi-purpose

Personal wikis are at the cutting edge of modern-day technology. With software developers competing globally for your business then acquiring one doesn't even have to be expensive. So, start thinking outside of the box and start looking at the potential of how having a personal wiki could transform your life! There is no end to what a personal wiki could do for you. It could schedule appointments, help you write your novel, project manage your home improvement project. Keep track of your personal finances.

Reason 2: It will reduce your stress levels

We all know that stress and pressure is no good for our heart. Not only that, when we are stressed then we are more likely to indulge in unhealthy lifestyle choices, for example eating fatty foods or drinking too much alcohol. Not having to worry about the minutia in your life will make things so much easier for you.

Reason 3: You can focus on what is important to you

Everyone has different ideas about what it means to relax. So, whether you want more time with your wife and kids, or would rather watch the game with your buddies having a personal wiki will make room in your life to ensure that this happens.

Maybe you hadn't even considered a personal wiki before now! Hopefully this article will serve as a stepping stone and help remove some of the stress from your life.

3 Reasons why Serendipity is a highly sought after commodity

Serendipity, or in other words a "happy surprise" is guaranteed to put a smile on the face of even the grizzliest of people. Let's face it who wouldn't want to come home to a candlelit dinner for two, or suddenly find themselves pregnant after struggling to conceive for several years. It is human nature to want to be loved and cherished and the concept of serendipity feeds nicely into that. So, for all of you happy, smiley people out there here are three reasons why serendipity is a highly sought after commodity:

Reason 1: It is associated with good luck

If you happen to be into chick flicks, then you will already know that serendipity is often associated with good luck and getting that elusive happily-ever-after. This is one of the many reasons why people want some of it in their lives. Because, if you can have one happy surprise, then maybe you can have ten, twenty or even hundreds of them!

Reason 2: It is priceless

If you were to put good luck into a bottle and then try and sell it, how much money do you think you would get for it? Well, with crazy bidding sites like EBay, then a conservative guess of millions of dollars probably wouldn't be too far off the mark. The world would be going crazy for it, and it sure would be a mighty genie in the bottle! How can you put a price on something like serendipity? Surely, it is priceless!

Reason 3: People crave their happily-ever after

For many the world can be a challenging place to live in. Even if you have managed to get lucky and find your dream partner and have a couple of gorgeous kids it can still be tough trying to make ends meet. Some serendipity would help life's problems disappear.

3 Reasons Why "Paying it Forward" Usually Pays off big time

The world in which we live has changed so much in recent years. More and more people are now "awakening" to a new way of doing things. However, is it really all so new? After all, didn't the bible preach the benefits of "Loving thy neighbor" Isn't the concept of paying it forward an old accepted wisdom that has been dressed up to make it fit in a more modern, contemporary world? If that has got you thinking, then here are 3 reasons why "Paying it forward" usually pays off big time.

Reason 1: You reap what you sow

While there are always going to be those who seem to constantly do misdeeds or trample over everyone else's feelings, there is a strong and compelling argument in the concept that you reap what you sow. At the risk of sounding too new age or spiritual, by paying it forward you raise your vibrations and the universe will generally reward you in kind. Sometimes you might get pay back immediately, other times it might take years for your good deed to reverberate in a way that is meaningful for you.

Reason 2: People will think you are someone they want to be with

When people see you being nice to others, it engenders a feel good factor. People will instinctively gravitate towards you and want to be with you. The great thing about this is as that good people generally gravitate towards fellow good people, so you should wind up with some really special, deep and meaningful relationships.

Reason 3: People will be more inclined to pay things forward for you

Once you start paying things forward, you should find that people start doing you small favors too. Human beings seem to be instinctively programed to copy and replicate behavior. So, good behavior and random acts of kindness should see you being rewarded in kind.

If nothing else, and if nothing good ever happens to you in return, you should still get a warm, buzzy feeling simply from knowing that you have helped make someone's life that little bit easier.

3 Reasons Why humans can't live forever

Why can't you live forever? The idea that immortality could somehow be magically possible seems to be a wish as old human civilization itself, but unfortunately - unless there's a secret that hasn't yet been disclosed to the public – human beings are stuck with being mortal.

Here are 3 reasons why humans can't live forever.

Reason 1: Bodies become weak.

Bodies become weaker the older they get. For one reason or another, whether it's to do with the brain or heart or any other necessary functioning part of the body, when the body ceases to operate, death is imminent! This is of course true for all types of life. What lives must die eventually.

Reason 2: Humans can't live forever, but what of the spirit?

Religious and spiritual people will believe that it's only the body that dies, whilst the spirit is indeed immortal! So if you look at things from a broader perspective than just science, it could be argued that humans can't live forever because their 'souls' are ready to move on!

Reason 3: Technological improvements.

Although human bodies are weak and more prone to disease the older they become, there are more and more advancements being made all the time. Organs can be replaced, stem cell research has helped to increase health, and all other manner of things. When you look at what's being done in the realms of Artificial Intelligence and robotics, perhaps in the future bodies will become so robust that death actually is possible to prevent! Maybe when human beings are made up of robotic organs and the like, immortality will be possible- but if this is the case, would human beings be human anymore?

However, if you are determined to achieve immortality yourself, your time may be better spent searching in ancient caves to see if you can find the Holy Grail or the elixir of life!

The 3 Reasons Why Book of Money & Business

3 Reasons Why babies learn things fast

Have you ever wondered why your toddler can easily navigate your IPad while you struggle to even switch it on? Or why babies take on board and process so much information in such a short space of time? Let's face it, they come out of the womb as these tiny, helpless little creatures and then within a matter of months they are walking, talking and wreaking havoc upon your world. Is this just a coincidence, do you think? Or is there a reason babies and toddlers seem to learn a gazillion times quicker than adults ever can.

Let's find out, here are 3 reasons why babies learn things fast.

Reason 1: Their prefrontal cortex is not fully developed

One of the most striking reasons why a baby might learn something a lot faster than say their thirty-year-old mom or dad is that their prefrontal cortex is also in its infancy. (This doesn't become fully developed until the child reaches adolescence) While this also is the reason for their, well, babyish behavior, the lack of prefrontal cortex means that their memory is much sharper. In other words, they can retain a lot more information than adults can. Whoever said that biology was boring!

Reason 2: It's a survival instinct

There has long since been a link between our empathetic connections to our ancient ancestors. Even though babies are born seemingly with no knowledge, on an instinctive level they understand that they need to learn to survive. Whereas a lot of adults, simply cannot be bothered to engage in the learning process, babies are little sponges just waiting to soak up and absorb the information as it is presented to them.

Reason 3: They aren't slowed down by life

Unlike adults who have to perform a multitude of tasks just to get through everyday life, babies are pretty much cocooned from the boring, banal stuff. Therefore, they have the time, and the mental "space" to be able devote to learning. Of course, they are not doing this on a conscious level. However, on a sub-conscious level that is precisely what they are doing.

So, next time you look at your toddler in complete bewilderment and question how on earth you could possibly have created such a genius, simply remember that psychologically you are at completely different places and in just a few short years, they will be as forgetful as you!

What do we stand to gain by knowing things? Take a look at some of the most successful people throughout history for the answer to that question: Abraham Lincoln, Henry Ford, Steve Jobs, Maya Angelou, Steven King and the list goes on. They all succeeded at their craft because they were highly knowledgeable in their field, as well as in life.

Knowledge is essential to success. It's a key component that drives people to succeed because the more knowledgeable an individual is, the more difficult it becomes to sit idly by and not put that knowledge into action. Knowledge often begets action. This is why having an educated community is essential to the improvement of any society. It all starts by picking up a book. Reading is a window into other worlds which allows people to gain essential knowledge, vicarious experience, imagination, creativity and much more. Here are three reasons why knowledge is essential.

Reason 1: Knowledge is power

Never forget that true power stems, not just from *knowing* things, but the way in which we utilize that knowledge. Conversely, ask yourself, what becomes of the uninformed individual? He is powerless to change his situation. Information is the cornerstone of change in both individuals and in society, and only by *knowing* things will we gain the power to change things.

How will you use your power of knowledge? At 3 Reasons Why, we believe in using knowledge to empower people everywhere. That's why we're hosting a series of events with knowledgeable guest speakers. Find the next 3RW event near you at events.3reasonswhy.com.

Reason 2: Knowledge is infectious

Have you ever learned something that you just had to share with another person? Knowledge is a fire that burns within us, begging to be released and spread from one person to the next. That is our mission here at 3RW – to spread knowledge to as many people as possible on as many topics as possible. Visit www.3ReasonsWhy.com and start spreading more knowledge today.

Reason 3: Knowledge is the remedy

Knowledge is the cure to poverty, because informed individual has an endless array of skills at his disposal which he uses to earn his keep. Knowledge is the cure to violence because the informed individual knows that there are alternative ways in which a conflict can be resolved. Knowledge is the cure to hunger, because the informed individual is resourceful and can find sustenance even in the harshest conditions. Knowledge is the remedy to most of life's little problems.

The world we live in is constantly in flux with an endless ebb and flow of information, all of which are made up of reasons that are ripe for *knowing*. As you walk down the crossroad of life, striving endlessly towards knowledge, there will undoubtedly be plenty of noise along the way. It can be easy to get distracted by the noise, but it is the task of every knowledge seeker to do their best to ignore that noise and find 3 simple reasons for everything.

Thank you or reading *The 3 Reasons Why Book of Money & Business*. If you enjoyed this book, you can find more reasons for just about everything at www.3ReasonsWhy.com. You can find more books like these available at books.3reasonswhy.com. Go forth and spread knowledge to the world.

www.ingramcontent.com/pod-product-compliance
Lightning Source LLC
Chambersburg PA
CBHW041500280526
45792CB00004B/1076